IMAGES

HISTORIC QUEENS COUNTY
Nova Scotia

TOM SHEPPARD

NIMBUS
PUBLISHING

Copyright © Tom Sheppard, 2001

All rights reserved. No part of this book may be reproduced, stored in a retrieval system or transmitted in any form or by any means without the prior written permission from the publisher, or, in the case of photocopying or other reprographic copying, permission from CANCOPY (Canadian Copyright Licensing Agency), 1 Yonge Street, Suite 1900, Toronto, Ontario M5E 1E5.

Nimbus Publishing Limited
PO Box 9166
Halifax, NS   B3K 5M8
(902) 455-4286

Design: Joan Sinclair

Printed and bound in Canada

Cover: Ships on the Liverpool waterfront, 1907.
Title page: Looking west along Liverpool's main street, 1890s.

National Library of Canada Cataloguing in Publication Data

Sheppard, Tom
        Historic Queens County, Nova Scotia

(Images of our past)
Includes bibliographical references.
ISBN 1-55109-384-7

        1. Queens (N.S.: County)—History. 2. Liverpool (N.S.)—History. I. Title.

FC2345.Q4S54 2001   971.6'24   C2001-902731-1
F1039.Q3S54 2001

We acknowledge the financial support of the Government of Canada through the Book Publishing Industry Development Program (BPIDP) and the Canada Council for our publishing activities.

For Sheila, Anne-Marie, and Jonathan

Acknowledgements

The photographs in this book have been collected from museums, archives, institutions and individuals. Some sources stand out in terms of their assistance. The Queens County Museum and its first-class research centre, named for author Thomas H. Raddall, have provided a significant amount of material. I thank curator Linda Rafuse and her staff for their friendly cooperation. Likewise, the North Queens Heritage House and its curator Sandra Rowter provided valuable assistance. Both the DesBrisay Museum in Bridgewater, with its curator Gary Selig, and the Public Archives of Nova Scotia in Halifax afforded me cooperation and assistance. I note particularly the help of Philip Hartling and Gary Shutlak, who offered their help at the public archives with unfailing good humour. I am also grateful to the South Shore Regional Library for the use of its local history collection and to the various branch workers who accommodated my requests.

Of the private individuals, I especially acknowledge the contributions of Tim McDonald, of Liverpool, who is something of a one-man historical industry in Queens County. Tim has not only amassed a large collection of historical photographs, many of which he has donated to the Queens County Museum, but he has prepared several works on local history for the museum, plus co-authored a book on the history of Milton. As well, I thank Peter Hope, chief interpreter at Kejimkujik National Park, who has organized a large collection of historical photographs for the park. Peter's uncompromisingly high standards about the proper crediting of photographs have always been kept in mind in the preparation of this book.

I relied extensively on the published and unpublished work of many people for whom history is a passion, including Mike Parker, who has written a number of the books in this series. I thank Nimbus Publishing for its commitment to this part of Canada. I also thank all of those who keep their old photographs, date and identify them where possible, and donate them to museums and archives. If a picture is worth a thousand words, their efforts have contributed immensely to the history of Nova Scotia.

Finally, of course, I acknowledge my wife, Sheila, whose skills as a proofreader have helped to polish the work in front of you. The errors are my own.

Contents

Introduction vii

CHAPTER 1
    The Communities of Queens: 1
    Town and Village Scenes

CHAPTER 2
    Landmarks Past and Present: 31
    Historic Homes and Important Buildings

CHAPTER 3
    The Sea and the Land: 61
    Fishing, Shipbuilding, Farming, Forestry, Mining,
    and Industry

CHAPTER 4
    Transportation—Getting About: 83
    Boats, Trains, Wagons, Automobiles

CHAPTER 5
    Daily Life: 101
    People, Schools, Stores, Churches, and Associations

CHAPTER 6
    Through Good Times and Bad: 133
    Sports, Leisure, Celebrations, and Historic Events

Image Sources 155

Bibliography 157

A note about the photographs and photographers

Wherever possible, I have tried to identify the photographer and the institution or person owning the photograph. The largest number of photographs came from the Queens County Museum, the North Queens Heritage House, the Tim McDonald collection, the Public Archives of Nova Scotia, Kejimkujik National Park and the DesBrisay Museum. Other photographs came from individuals, including Carol Doggett, White Point; Hilda Harper, North Brookfield; Blair Douglas, Caledonia; Marilyn Clarke, East Port L'Hebert; Harry Ball, Hibernia; Eugene Penney, Caledonia; Bill Wamboldt, Greenfield; Laura Wamboldt, Greenfield; Beryl Berringer, South Brookfield; Alan Wilson, Northwest Cove; Mary Lee Mahoney, New Grafton; Judy Cole, Rosette Road; Shirley Smith, Harmony; and Freda Smith, South Brookfield.

Because of the depth and quality of the Queens County Museum collection and the Tim McDonald collection, I relied less on private donors when collecting material for South Queens. Many of the community's historical photographs have been donated to the museum and are catalogued there. I tried to achieve a rough balance among the many communities of Queens County in order to tell the whole county's story, and where a community is left out of one chapter it appears in another. Sometimes the simple availability or non-availability of photographs dictated the prominence given to a particular community. I note the work of early photographers such as N.D. Hammett, Liverpool; Gilbert Kempton, Liverpool; Alister Harlow, Milton; L.G. Swain, Yarmouth and Caledonia; Paul Yates, Digby; and Les Henley, Caledonia, all of whose photographs are in this book. It is almost certain that L.G. Swain took some of the photographs of the gold mines.

Introduction

In 1873 it was said of Queens County that there was not a county in the province more eminently endowed with natural advantages. Historian James F. More wrote that every river abounded with fish, the forests contained a rich assortment of timber for shipbuilding and exporting, and fertile soils "clothed a portion" of its surface.

The county he spoke of so fondly lies in the southwestern part of Nova Scotia, with Lunenburg County on the east and Shelburne County on the west. There is a point on its interior boundary that touches Shelburne, Yarmouth, and Digby counties, and the northern border with Annapolis County begins just a short distance from there. The southern part of the county is coastal, with villages and towns connected to the sea. In the north, the villages are nestled among forests, rivers, and lakes. Not only does the largest freshwater lake in the province lie within the county's boundaries, but so too does the largest concentration of lakes in Nova Scotia. The land is so wild and so beautiful that significant portions of Queens County are both a national park and a provincial wildlife area—the largest wilderness area in the Maritime region. The south contains a seaside adjunct to the national park, plus a provincial camping park.

This book is a record of life in Queens County, told through historic photographs. On July 21, 1762, the County of Queens was formally proclaimed, with all of the territory including the townships of Liverpool, Barrington and Yarmouth placed in one county, Liverpool being the shire-town. This book, however, focuses on the area enclosed by present-day boundaries. Much of the story is told through the photographs and the accompanying captions, but the focus is always on communities, because communities developed in an outward direction from Liverpool and remain the key to the story of Queens County. And it starts where it must start, with the community of the Mi'kmaq.

THE MI'KMAQ

The human history of Queens County begins with the Mi'kmaq. While the sea brought explorers to the coast of Queens County and was responsible for the establishment of Liverpool in 1759, the Mi'kmaq lived on the lands and waters of what was to become Queens County for well over four thousand years. The history of the Mi'kmaq is an oral history, passed down through the generations, an unbroken thread connecting the people of today to their ancestors. It is impossible to overlook the way the Mi'kmaq cared for the land, extracting whatever resources were needed, thanking the spirits for what was provided, and always trying to give something back.

A complex social system based on the concepts of sharing, cooperation, and respect for the natural world characterized the Mi'kmaq society that existed long before European settlers arrived. It was a society that would find it hard to understand our political boundaries, since the local Mi'kmaq ranged over the whole of southwestern Nova Scotia. This was a hunting and gathering society. The Mi'kmaq would travel from the Fundy coast to the Atlantic coast as the seasons and food dictated, using corridors provided by the lakes and rivers of the inland region.

Among the areas where the Mi'kmaq established encampments was the site of the future town of Liverpool, which they called *Ogomkegea*. As well, a few kilometres upriver was the important community later known as Indian Gardens. The river, which served as a major highway for the Mi'kmaq, was later called the Mersey. This thriving community fell victim to the collision between European and native peoples. In 1928, due to the construction of a power dam, much of the area occupied by the Mi'kmaq was covered by water. There were also important Mi'kmaq sites throughout the northern part of the county, centred partly on the area now known as Kejimkujik National Park.

**MATTIO JEREMY,
MI'KMAQ HUNTER AND TRAPPER**

The legendary Mi'kmaq hunter and trapper Mattio Jeremy, who grew up in the Kejimkujik Lake area of the Northern District, is shown in this 1913 photograph from the Public Archives of Nova Scotia. The photographer, Edward Breck, noted that it was from Mattio Jeremy's family name that Jeremy's Bay, now a part of Kejimkujik National Park, received its name.

In early European accounts, the Mi'kmaq were wrongly described as savages. This stemmed partly from the alliance the Mi'kmaq had made with the French in Nova Scotia during their wars with the English. As in all wars, there were incidents of brutality on both sides. In reality, the Mi'kmaq had developed a sophisticated social system. Mi'kmaq political life was democratic. There was a system of districts, each district being made up of villages. Mi'kmaq writer Mike Sack has said that "each district chose a chief for his ability to lead men and inspire confidence, his territorial knowledge, his understanding of the seasonal habits of animals and his skill as a good spokesman." The economy was fundamentally co-operative, based on a quest for food. History was remembered through stories, which were a celebrated part of life; sometimes storytelling would go on for days.

The Mi'kmaq gave us the canoe, which in many ways has become the symbol of Kejimkujik National Park. Interpreters from the park tell visitors that the best way to see it is by canoe. The actual name of the park is now Kejimkujik National Park and National Historic Site of Canada, the latter portion of the name having been added recently to honour the Mi'kmaq ancestors who first used the land, with the official plaque being unveiled in 2000. The plaque refers to the fact that the Mi'kmaq had a presence in Kejimkujik "since time immemorial."

NEW ENGLAND SETTLERS ESTABLISH LIVERPOOL

At the time when Liverpool was settled, Halifax was ten years old and its first newspaper, first also in Canada, had been publishing for only seven years. The Acadians, proudly refusing to sign an oath of allegiance to England, had been expelled from Nova Scotia just four years before, an outcome of the struggle between England and France for control of North America. Lunenburg had been settled six years before by people of Germanic extraction and was a struggling farming and fishing community, while Annapolis Royal, founded as Port Royal in 1605, had since become little more than a military outpost. The Fortress of Louisburg, symbol of French power in North America, had fallen to the English just the year before.

The year was 1759. Prior to that the coastal areas around what was to become Liverpool had been visited by European fishermen, but it was New England that provided the people who founded the first permanent settlement. Bruce Fergusson, former Provincial Archivist of Nova Scotia, wrote that Liverpool was substantially colonized by descendants of the first Plymouth and Puritan settlers, who came from Cape Cod, Plymouth, and adjacent towns. "Liverpool rose," he said, "from the efforts made, after the deportation of the Acadians, to fill up the vacant and the vacated lands of the Province, and from the interest evoked in New England by the inducements offered to prospective settlers. For a time, however, the attractiveness of the opportunities was offset by temporary disadvantages. It took four years to get a favourable response and an additional year before the migration really began. The founding of Liverpool was a part of the wave of immigration from the colonies to the south."

In 1759, four men applied for a grant to settle a township at what was to become Liverpool. By fall, Governor Charles Lawrence had issued John Doggett, Elisha Freeman, Samuel Doggett, and Thomas Foster a preliminary grant to establish the township. All of these names exist in Queens County today. At the same time, Lawrence issued grants to establish townships such as Horton, Cornwallis, Falmouth, Granville, and Annapolis. By September of the next year, it was expected that fifty families would be settled in the township of Liverpool.

The first settlers from Plymouth landed in May 1760, though there were a few others at nearby Port Lawrence, from the winter before. The first year the settlers were busy laying out the township, running the lines and choosing lots for shelter. Affairs had to be organized so that the development of the community would be orderly, with homes, sawmills, barns, storehouses, and fish houses constructed. Gardens had to be planted and fishing begun. Cattle feed had to be stored for the coming winter.

A year later, Liverpool was being described as the boom town of North America. In August, the townships of Liverpool, Barrington, and Yarmouth were set up as a single county, and given the name of Queens, with Liverpool as the county seat. Milton historian Francis Freeman Tupper wrote that there was an extraordinary number of captains living in the town in the early years, an indication of the popularity of the town. "Captains would be much in evidence around the Liverpool taverns," he wrote in *Historic Liverpool*. "On a propitious day the chambermaid who emptied the slops out the upstairs window might flush a covey of them at any time. With any luck she might be able to get three and even five captains at one shot."

There were severe food shortages that winter, but by the end of the year it could be reported that Liverpool had ninety families, more than five hundred people in all, earning their living by fishing and forestry. Fergusson quotes a description of the settlement at the time:

> They have built Seventy Houses, have employed Seventeen Schooners in the Fishery and made about eight thousand Quintals of Fish besides which they have made a considerable quantity of Shingles, Clapboards, Staves, and effected a sawmill for Sawing boards. The Township comprehends the Lands lying on the Ocean from: Port Metway four miles west of the River, and Harbour of Port Senior; The Harbour is Barr'd having but Nine feet at low-water, but safe and convenient within the River, and good Anchoring in three fathom; The Country and Soil much the same with Lunenburg, abounds more with Oak and some Pine. High and mountainous within Land…

So Liverpool grew and prospered. We have a good account of what life was like in Liverpool during its early days because of the Simeon Perkins diaries. Perkins arrived in Liverpool just three years after it was founded to seek his fortune away from his home in Connecticut, where his young wife had died just two weeks after the birth of their son. He was twenty-seven when he arrived, built a home which is now a part of the Queens County

Museum, kept a diary, and engaged in all manner of activities, from keeping stores to owning sawmills and engaging in privateering. Very soon after he arrived, Perkins became a member of the proprietors' committee that governed Liverpool, a position he held for thirty-two years. He was town treasurer, a justice of the peace, and a justice of the Inferior Court of Common Pleas. He was appointed Commissioner of Roads, a judge of probate, Lieutenant-Colonel of the Militia of Queens County and then Commandant, and was an elected representative from Queens County to the Legislative Assembly of Nova Scotia.

In all of this he found time to marry again, this time to a widow, Elizabeth Young Headly, who had a daughter of her own. They eventually had six daughters and two sons. Thomas H. Raddall, one of Canada's best-loved novelists and historians, said that Simeon Perkins was destined to be the heart and soul of the new settlement of Liverpool in the stormy years to come, and the historian of its early struggles. Raddall was foremost in the effort to have Simeon Perkins' home made into a museum, and in the neat completion of a circle, the Queens County Museum, next to Perkins House, today houses the Thomas H. Raddall Research Centre, which includes a reconstruction of the study in which Raddall wrote.

The stormy times referred to by Raddall had to do, of course, with privateering. Privateers were vessels which received letters of marque from the governing authorities, allowing them to arm themselves and both protect their home coastlines and harass enemy shipping. For many of the years after its settlement, Liverpool and privateering were inextricably linked. Liverpool was one of the most important ports for shipping and shipbuilding in eastern Canada and the most legendary privateers sailed out of its harbour. Sylvanus Cobb, who built a home in Liverpool just after the settlement was founded, captained a privateer vessel as early as 1744. Cobb, whose Liverpool house was destroyed by fire in 1945, was thought to be the captain of the ship that landed General Wolfe during the siege of Quebec.

After the American Revolution there was little love lost between New England seafaring men and the people of Nova Scotia, who were to some degree allied with the king, though many still thought the province should become the fourteenth colony. American privateers made raids on ships and communities along the Nova Scotia coast, and to strike back, Liverpool commissioned a schooner, the *Enterprise*, to protect shipping. Captained by Joseph Barss (senior), with one of its largest shareholders being Simeon Perkins, the *Enterprise* set off from Liverpool Harbour and returned after twelve days, having captured twelve vessels, thereby turning the tables on the American privateers. That was just the beginning. From then on storied vessels like the *Lord Nelson*, the *Lord Spencer*, the *Rover* and the *Charles*

Mary Wentworth engaged in privateering, becoming the scourge of American ships. To this day, the privateering history of Liverpool is celebrated each year with the Privateer Days festival.

Privateering, shipping and shipbuilding caused Liverpool to prosper. During the war of 1812, according to Janet Mullins, who wrote about Liverpool history and privateering in the 1930s, fifty private armed vessels were fitted out in Liverpool—a new generation of famous ships, with names like the *Retaliation*, the *Shannon*, and the *Liverpool Packet*. Mullins calls the *Liverpool Packet* the greatest privateer of all time. Captained by Joseph Barss (junior), "She is said to have made two hundred captures, fifty of which were brought before the Court of Vice-Admiralty." The *Liverpool Packet* revolutionized the way sea traffic was conducted along the Atlantic coasts and even sparked the idea of building a canal across Cape Cod so that other ships could avoid so effective a privateer.

Liverpool had a congregational meeting house by 1765, the Old Zion church by 1775, a school in place by 1777, and a post office in operation by 1802. Through much of the 1800s, Liverpool was a busy, wealthy town,

LIVERPOOL'S MAIN STREET, 1886

Liverpool's main street runs along the south side of Liverpool Harbour, about a block from the waterfront. This view, looking west, was taken in 1886 and shows the steeples of the Baptist Church, rebuilt after the great fire of 1865, and the Congregational Church, built in 1865 (now Zion United). The open area with trees to the left of the photograph is the Old Burial Ground, earliest cemetery in Liverpool. The photograph is in the Tim McDonald collection.

one of the most important in the province, with large, lovely homes and tree-lined streets. Thomas Chandler Haliburton, in 1829, called it the best-built town in Nova Scotia. Thomas Raddall said that "during the prime of 'wooden ships and iron men,' Liverpool was busy launching windjammers and sending them in the carrying trade around the world." Photographers like N.D. Hammett and Gilbert Kempton began recording the life of the town in pictures, and their work helps to carry forward the rest of the story.

SETTLEMENT EXPANDS BEYOND LIVERPOOL

The settlement of Queens County moved in something of an arc from Liverpool, though coastal villages such as Port Mouton and Port Medway were growing up almost at the same time. The village of Brooklyn is adjacent to Liverpool, and today is the site of the most important industry in the county, the Bowater Mersey Paper Company. It is also the site of the first European attempt to put down roots in Queens County, since French explorers Nicholas Denys and Isaac de Razilly established a shore fishery there in the 1630s. It proved to be short-lived, however, and permanent settlement was established with the arrival of the New England settlers. The Mi'kmaq called the area *Katkootch*, meaning "between the hills," and used it extensively as a seasonal camping ground, partly to trade with French adventurers. It also went by the name of Herring Cove. The first sawmill was established by Ichabod Darrow, and by 1873 there were a gang mill, sawmill, and box factory.

Milton is just up the Mersey River from Liverpool and was settled quickly, since the great river which had its headwaters near Annapolis provided a source of energy to saw the lumber needed to build the community. For years to come, mills would be the lifeblood of Milton, at one time called The Falls. The first sawmill was established in 1760 on the west side of the river and was bought out by Simeon Perkins three years later. At one time or another there were mills owned by men with names like Freeman, Nickerson, Coops, Brown, Ellis, Cole, Kempton, Ford, Dexter, Tupper, Burnaby, Harlow, Millard, Minard, Morton, Collins, Hartlen, McLeod, and MacLeod. Small wonder that the village became known as Milton.

Port Medway is at the eastern edge of Queens County, near the Lunenburg County border and at the mouth of the Medway River, the other major river that runs down through Queens County to the sea. The Mi'kmaq called the area *Ulgwedook*, or "place of mushrooms." According to Marguerite Letson's delightful history of Port Medway, *Port: A Short History of Port Medway, Nova Scotia*, Champlain is thought to have referred to the port when he spoke of Port Maltois, and it is reasonable to assume, Letson writes, that the current name is a corruption of that. Simeon Perkins and others referred to it as Port Metway, with Metway gradually changing to Medway. The Public Archives of Nova Scotia, in a reference work prepared as a centennial year project on place names, suggests that Port Medway may be a variation of Port Midway, since the settlement was approximately midway between Bridgewater and Liverpool.

Permanent settlement of the area began with the arrival of the New England settlers in 1760, carrying on a fairly prosperous fishery. Because of its location at the mouth of a river running through virgin forest, lumbering was an important industry; moreover, there was a shipbuilding industry that enabled merchants to send off the lumber which they milled a short distance from town.

Soon after arriving in Port Medway, men from the village moved upriver—just as they had done in Liverpool—and built a sawmill at what was to become Mill Village. Simeon Perkins was among eight men who

THE OLD MEETING HOUSE, PORT MEDWAY

This photograph shows the interior of the old meeting house, Port Medway. The building was erected around 1832 by the Free Christian Baptists, a sect that came to Nova Scotia with the Loyalists. The building is unique in that there is a central aisle, with the seats rising on each side of the aisle, the people in the pews facing each other. In earlier times the women were said to have sat on one side of the church (the side on the right in the photograph) and the men on the other. This photograph was taken by E.G.L. Wetmore in 1953 and is in the Public Archives.

built the mill, which was bought out by Samuel Mack eight years later. The village is about fifteen kilometres northeast of Liverpool and has also been called both Mills Village and Port Mills, references to the saw and grist mills located on the river. The first settlers to establish the mills were Smith and Mosely, who sold their mills to Samuel Mack in 1764.

Mack, like many of the other founders of Liverpool, had come from Connecticut. At that time the chief clerk for Simeon Perkins' lumber business was Patrick Doran, who was born in Waterford, Ireland. Doran went to work for Samuel Mack, also as chief clerk, and when Samuel Mack died, Doran married his widow, Desire. One of their daughters married a Davison. E.D. Davison, destined to become one of Nova Scotia's most important sawmill owners, was born in the house built by Samuel Mack's widow.

There are a number of other small communities in this area. Charleston is about six kilometres up the Medway River from Mill Village. The Mi'kmaq called it *Banoo*, "the first lake on the river." In the 1870s, a pulp mill was established at Charleston, which burned in 1905 and was then rebuilt.

Eagle Head is near the north eastern side of Queens County, at the head of Eagle Head Bay. It was settled by descendants of the Liverpool settlers. Beach Meadows is near Eagle Head, just east of Liverpool. One of the proprietors, Joseph Woods, settled in Beach Meadows before 1795. The communities of Puddingpan and Blueberry were nearby, eastward along the coast from Eagle Head. Puddingpan is today called East Berlin, and Blueberry is called West Berlin, so named because the settlers, of German extraction, couldn't decide whether to name a school built more than 130 years ago on the border between Puddingpan and Blueberry after the one community or the other. Consequently, they called the area Berlin, East and West. Today an island off shore still bears the name Puddingpan.

South of Liverpool, at the mouth of Liverpool Bay, is Western Head, settled by 1829 by Germans who had come from Lunenburg. A newspaper account published in Boston in 1897 said of Western Head that "the pedestrian or cyclist cannot go astray in quest of beautiful scenery." Next to Western Head is Moose Harbour, opened up soon after Liverpool by black settlers from New England. Both Moose Harbour and Western Head were ravaged by a forest fire in 1955 which destroyed houses, businesses, and fishing boats.

To the west of Liverpool lies White Point, named for the white sand beaches and now home to a major year-round resort and a golf course. It was opened in 1802, when Ebenezer West built his home there. Close by is Hunt's Point. The land around Hunt's Point was granted to Deacon Samuel Hunt in 1788, hence its name. Michael Hupman, who descended from the Lunenburg County Germans, bought the land from Hunt in 1813; his name lives on in the names of those in the area. Then comes Summerville Beach, settled by 1787 by John Collins, and now an important tourist destination, thanks to its spectacular beach.

Port Mouton on the western side of Port Mouton Bay was settled at approximately the same time as Liverpool. Long before its founding, however, the Mi'kmaq called it *Wologumk*, meaning a deep gully or hole in the river. M. Marie Woodworth, who wrote a history of Port Mouton, said that the Mi'kmaq would camp along the shores of the area, fishing, digging clams, and gathering bird's eggs. The French carried on a fishery in the area for 150 years, and in 1759 fishermen were establishing a settlement at what was to be Port Mouton. There were no roads, of course, with homes being built along the shore. Some of the earliest names—Doggett, McLearn and Stewart—can be found in their descendants today.

In 1783, disbanded soldiers under the command of Sir Guy Carleton settled in Port Mouton, in a properly-laid out township six kilometres long and seventeen kilometres deep, with blocks of land separated by roadways and containing common lands for the use of all. On October 10, 1783, the first of the Loyalists arrived: 125 men and 175 women and children. Throughout that month and November, two thousand more arrived. They had a terrible winter with many dying of exposure. The next spring, a forest fire destroyed most of the buildings, and the Loyalists were ready to settle elsewhere. Most went on to what became Guysborough County. Port Mouton carried on, however. By the close of the eighteen hundreds it was reported that fishermen were living in snug houses around the harbour and that there was a hotel.

Port Joli lies just west of Port Mouton, at the head of Port Joli Bay. By 1786 a road had been pushed through from Liverpool to Shelburne, further opening up this area. A hundred years ago, Port Joli was described as a thrifty fishing and farming village, with a rugged shore "that invites us to hear what the wild waves are saying." The Mi'kmaq called it *Emsik*, meaning "blown along by the wind." Its origins were similar to those of Port Mouton, with settlement beginning in the early 1760s and being swelled by Loyalists twenty years later.

On the edge of Queens County next to Shelburne County is the tiny community of Port L'Hebert. Strictly speaking, the area is East Port L'Hebert, since the other half of the village, West Port L'Hebert, is in Shelburne County. The French used to call the area Port of Bears—Port Aux Ours—but it came to be known as Port Hebert. The assumption was made that Champlain had named it after Louis Hebert. It was settled soon after Liverpool and was divided in two when Shelburne County was established in 1784.

The Northern District

While the coastal area had been settled for forty years, the inland area to the north was still known mainly to the Mi'kmaq. Robert Randall McLeod, the bard of Queens County, put it beautifully when he wrote in *Acadiensis* in 1904 that the Indians:

> had named all the lakes and streams in their smooth, sweet tongue, and were at home in the dim aisles of the great coniferous forests that hemmed in the lonely lakes, and by the borders of streams that glided in shine and shadow of meadows' margins and the coverts of birches and beeches, maples and oaks and alders.

The lack of attention paid to the interior of Queens County ended with William Burke and Joseph Gloade. Burke, who had been born on a voyage from England to Nova Scotia when Liverpool was just four years old and whose father had been a blacksmith in Halifax, was adopted by Samuel Mack of Mill Village when Burke's father died. As he grew up, Burke was friendly with the Mi'kmaq who lived around Mill Village, and, as McLeod tells us, they took him into the northern wilderness on their hunting trips. They went north by canoe along the Medway River. Burke was struck by the beauty of the region and by the hardwood hills, which he knew could support good farms. His friend and companion Joseph Gloade was a Mi'kmaq, very much at home in the forests of the Northern District. He and Burke went together "up the river to the beautiful oasis that lay bounded with the great evergreen forests." Gloade too saw the potential of the meadows and drumlins—fertile hills left behind by glaciers—of the area.

Burke married Mary Foster, the daughter of Edward Foster, of Liverpool. At the age of twenty he moved to Milton, where he decided he wanted to see the Milton road extended to the other side of the province. When a group of men from Nictaux, in Annapolis County, walked through the woods to petition for a road, Burke quickly gave his support. In the end, a group from Liverpool and another from Nictaux agreed to blaze half the trail each. This took place in 1798 and a year later Burke built a log cabin at South Brookfield, on a knoll with a brook, meadows, and surrounding hills. With the help of Joseph Gloade, Burke, Mary, and their four children made the move. The place they chose grew to be the present-day community of South Brookfield, which recently had a celebration on the site to mark its 200th birthday.

While no other settlers rushed to join them, the Burkes were able to survive with the assistance of Joseph Gloade, who hovered close by with his own family. Fairly soon after, a succession of others settled in the Northern District, most of them moving inland from Liverpool. Within two years a man named James Daley, originally from Shelburne but living in Port

Medway, joined Burke in South Brookfield. In fairly rapid order, families with names like Freeman, Carder and Waterman moved inland. In 1804 an English sea captain named Thomas Christopher established a farm at South Brookfield; today, a lovely chain of lakes—the Christopher Lakes—bears his name. Fosters, Minards, Harlows, McLeods, and Hunts all followed.

The village of Caledonia, centre of services for the Northern District today, was settled close to 1817. The best evidence is that six (or seven) Scots and one (or two) Irishmen, the majority of whom were single, each chose a drumlin for a farm, giving rise to the expression "Seven settlers, seven hills." R.R. McLeod tells us that they were industrious men, including among them two stone masons, two carpenters, and two wheelwrights. They were Alexander Spears, Andrew McLeod, Allen McLean, John Douglas, Richard Telfer, George Middlemas, his brother, David Middlemas, and Edward Hayes.

When the settlers arrived they built a log house on a cove by the shores of a little lake and all lived there together while they built their own homesteads. The house became known as Scotch House. James Morrison and Lawrence Friend, who wrote a history of the interior of southwestern Nova Scotia, say that Scotch House was built by the group for George Middlemas, since he was the only married man (although it appears that Richard and Mary Telfer were married by this time, too). The settlers spent the winter in Scotch House, going out during the days to clear land on their farms, cut logs and build their own houses. George was married to Margaret Douglas, a sister of John Douglas. If the job of cooking for all of the men fell to Margaret Middlemas and Mary Telfer, it is well to reflect that their names should be listed among the first settlers. Mary Telfer arrived in what was to become Caledonia, riding on a feather bed strapped to a horse.

Others quickly moved in. Ten years later, Benjamin Annis and his wife Lavinia Morine, originally from Liverpool, moved close to Caledonia to a place called Hibernia and established a farm. The village of Caledonia grew quickly in size and importance, so that much of the old road from Liverpool through Brookfield and on to Nictaux became secondary to the road which ran through Caledonia and on up to Annapolis. Caledonia became the centre for services, the location of the major hotels, stores, a newspaper, stagecoach stops, and a bank, and a few years later was described in reports as the gateway to the fisherman's, hunter's and sportsman's paradise of the Northern District. It became the centre for services required by the gold rush, which began in the 1800s. School was being taught by James Brydon in 1829, a Roman Catholic church was built in 1836, a post office was established by 1855, and a newspaper in 1888.

At this point, communities were growing in all directions in the Northern District. On the eastern edge of the northern part of the county lay Pleasant River, settled by Zenas Waterman in October 1802. It was said of Zenas that he knew how to build good roads—none of that throwing of sod into the roadway—and that it was he who rebuilt the road from the Northern District to Liverpool, changing it from a footpath that went from summit to summit to a road that avoided those obstacles. Some settlers came from the other direction, moving south from Annapolis County. Another early inhabitant was Samuel Hunt, son of one of the original proprietors of Liverpool, who set up shop in Pleasant River as a cooper and dealer in liquid spirits.

Samuel Hunt used to visit the area around what is now Greenfield and recognized its potential. The Mi'kmaq called the beautiful lake that defines the Greenfield area, plus the area itself, *Ponoque*, from which we get today's name of Ponhook Lake. "Ponoque" roughly means the outlet from the first lake on the river. One description of the settlement of the area notes that the Mi'kmaq had already cleared some land in the area when the first settlers arrived, and were not especially friendly to people who would take over their land, so the settlers moved a little further along to a place they called Wellington.

Hunt, however, prevailed. As described in a manuscript prepared by Janet Wile in the summer of 1830,

> he and his wife, Lucerna, and their six children put all their effects on a two-wheeled wooden cart and hauled them to a spot on Ponoque Lake, now known as Cameron's Landing. Here they loaded their belongings into rowboats and rowed to Greenfield. They landed on the east side of the river just above the falls and built a log cabin. Later, they built a frame house from the boards that composed his cooper's shop in Pleasant River.

Decades after, a ferry service followed the same route from Cameron's Landing to Greenfield.

Samuel and Lucerna had the first child born to a settler in Greenfield in 1832, a daughter they named Lois. They eventually had 12 children and 68 grandchildren, and Hunt is still a local name. The second house in Greenfield was built by Gorham Freeman, another surname important today. In 1832 Freeman built an up-and-down sawmill. The community grew. Greenfield had a postal way office in 1857, a Baptist church by 1862, and a school house by 1873. Milling, both lumber and grist, sustained the community then and still does—the Harry Freeman and Sons lumber mill is today one of the largest employers in Queens County.

Eventually, tourism began to shoulder its way in as a significant economic activity. By the turn of the century, Greenfield was one of the areas in the Northern District known as a fishing and hunting paradise, with New England providing many of the visitors to use local guides.

About halfway between Liverpool and South Brookfield is the community of Middlefield, settled in the early 1800s by James Morton and Zenas

THE LITTLE RIVERSIDE CHURCH AT BANGS FALLS, NEAR GREENFIELD

Measuring only 18 by 24 feet, this little church sits beside the Medway River in the village of Bangs Falls, just outside Greenfield. The photograph was taken in the 1930s by Clara Dennis (daughter of Senator William Dennis), who travelled Nova Scotia and New Brunswick writing a series of articles for her father's newspaper, The Halifax Herald. *The church was built in late 1907 and early 1908 at the instigation of Halifax lawyer John Y. Payzant, who often visited the nearby hunting and fishing lodge Bangscote. Payzant was the uncle of Rev. Harry Y. Payzant, the church's first minister and the minister of the United Baptist Church in Greenfield. In 1912, the little church, which has never had electricity, had thirty-six children in its Sunday school, but by the 1950s it had fallen into disuse. In 1989, a group of community volunteers, led by Marilyn Fraser, Margie Joudrey, Betty Peach, Jack Veinot, and Kevin and Marsha Freeman, restored the church. Today it sits open for visitors in its spot by the river and is used a few times a year for services and weddings, earning the title informally bestowed upon it by the newspapers as the province's "cutest church." The bridge in the photograph was built in the early 1900s.*

Waterman, both of whom received a grant to build an inn for the people travelling between Liverpool and the Northern District. Morton was said to have lived in the eastern side of the house, and Waterman—before he resumed farming in Pleasant River—on the western side. The inn was near the site where the county poor farm was constructed in 1894. Hillsview Acres, a home for seniors, is located there now.

Further north on the same road, on the other side of Caledonia, is Harmony, or Harmony Mills, settled in 1821 by men with names like Cushing, Kempton, Harlow, and Freeman. It was a vibrant community, supported by sawmills, grist mills, logging, farming and gold mining. Kempt is next, heading toward the Annapolis County border. It was settled at approximately the same time as Caledonia and Harmony by Francis, Richard and Thomas Kempton, whose surname, coupled with a visit by Lieutenant Governor Sir James Kempt in 1822, left the community with its name. Today Kempt is a pretty little community perhaps best known for its outstanding community suppers.

NORTH BROOKFIELD GOLD MINE NEAR THE END OF THE NINETEENTH CENTURY

Beneath the majestic pines and tranquil lakes of the Northern District men found gold in the 1880s, sparking an economic boom that made the area one of the most important mining regions of the province. The gold rush was relatively short-lived, but while it lasted it provided a source of income for many people, including these men who worked in the North Brookfield gold mine around 1900. This photograph is from the North Queens Heritage House.

The village of Westfield is west of South Brookfield, along the Medway River. Its settlement was tied to the settlement of South Brookfield around 1822, with mills and farms being developed by such people as James Daley (the name eventually became Dailey) and James Bent McLeod, father of Robert Randall McLeod, the writer and naturalist. The descendants of James Daley ran an important mill in Westfield on the Rosette Road, and a gold mine, the Jumbo Mine, opened in the 1880s, employing many of the men of the village.

Finally, one of the most attractive villages in the county is New Grafton, tucked off the main highway and next to the border with Annapolis County. At one time it was the main entrance to the lakes, cabins, and lodges of the Kedgemakooge Country. It was settled in 1821 by Scots, who gave the area its name.

Some of the communities in the Northern District are ghosts of their former selves. The population of Molega Mines is small these days, and that of Whiteburn almost nonexistent, whereas after the discovery of gold in the 1880s they were busy mining communities with stores, hotels, schools, houses, taverns, dance halls, and populations of between five hundred and twelve hundred people. R.R. McLeod said in *Markland,* his comprehensive history of Nova Scotia, that "a succession of pretty villages extend over this region, that is known as the 'Northern District.' " He said that "fine farms, orchards, and mills, and good houses are everywhere in evidence of the fair prosperity of the inhabitants. The whole region is convenient to excellent hunting grounds of moose and small game, and streams for trout fishing."

Chapter 1

The Communities of Queens

TOWN AND VILLAGE SCENES

AERIAL PHOTOGRAPH OF LIVERPOOL AND MILTON, 1946

Liverpool is the county seat for Queens and contains the largest concentration of its population. This aerial photograph, taken by the Royal Canadian Air Force in 1946, shows the buildings of the town of Liverpool clustered around the end of Liverpool Harbour. The Mersey River, which flows into the harbour and which in the early years was called the Great River, is one of the largest rivers in Nova Scotia and has its headwaters just south of Annapolis Royal. The Mi'kmaq used it as a passageway between the Fundy and South shores. The bridge over the Mersey is seen to the right of the harbour, and the railway bridge can be seen at the upper portion of the harbour with the village of Milton beyond.

BRIDGE AT LIVERPOOL, 1890

This photograph shows an iron drawbridge built in 1888 across the harbour at Liverpool with a sign at the top saying "Walk your horse or you will be fined." A wooden toll bridge once crossed the harbour charging foot passengers one cent to cross, wheelbarrow and man two cents, a single horse and driver seven cents, a pair of horses and driver ten cents, a horse and rider six cents, and a yearly toll for carriages amounting to five pounds. At the town end of the toll bridge, writes Janet E. Mullins in her *Chronicles of Liverpool*, were four bars which sold liquor. At the opposite end was a point of land where later there was a shipyard owned by Captain Lewis Sponagle, not far from the Joseph Barss house, which is today an inn. The bridge was gated, one for carriages and teams and one for foot passengers, and was lit by lanterns at the gates.

The toll bridge was removed in 1867 and another erected at a cost of $20,000. That bridge was replaced in 1888 by the bridge in the photograph, with one span having the capacity of being opened so that boats could pass through and go up the river. The newspaper of September 11, 1889 said: "Liverpool New Bridge was built and finished last December by John Stewart, Esq., of New Glasgow. It is a beautiful structure of iron with wooden flooring, a swinging section and piers of wood to which vessels may fasten until ready to drop through." It said that the draw on the bridge could be worked by a boy of six, it was so easy to work. "There could be no more handsome mode of entrance to our town." The photograph was taken by Gilbert Kempton and is in the collection of the Queens County Museum.

LIVERPOOL'S INNER HARBOUR, 1895

This photograph was taken from a church steeple in 1895. It shows in the foreground Liverpool's inner harbour and the harbour bridge in the centre of the picture. The turntable span on the bridge can be seen on its right. Shipyard Point, where Simeon Perkins (among others), built ships, is just out of the picture on the lower left.

When the railway came, its bridge across the Mersey was also built with a span which could be cranked open. John Morton, diarist, wrote in April 1908 that the first vessel since construction had begun on the railroad bridge had come up river to load lumber at his wharf, though strong currents had made the passage dangerous. The fate of the harbour and river as navigable bodies of water was sealed in 1960 when a new vehicle bridge was built. Despite the pleas of local politicians, the government refused to build a bridge that could be opened to allow vessels through. Ships could no longer use the inner harbour or the river. A process of filling in the waterfront began, so that the area in the photograph which shows wharves stretching out into the water is now a parking lot and park, and the inner harbour lies empty.

THE BARSS-GARDNER SHIPYARD, NEXT TO WHAT IS NOW LANE'S PRIVATEER INN, C.1890S

This view from the bridge in Liverpool looking toward the Bristol Avenue side shows the Barss-Gardner Shipyard. The location was next to the site of Captain Joseph Barss's home, now occupied by Lane's Privateer Motor Inn, which sports a Captain Barss Lounge. While today the area occupied by the shipyard is lawn, trees, a boat ramp, and parking for the inn, throughout Liverpool's history it was occupied by different shipyards producing sailing ships for world trade and privateering.

SCHOONER LOADED WITH LUMBER WITH THE NEW TOWN HALL IN THE BACKGROUND, C.1905

This photograph of a white three-masted schooner docked on the Liverpool waterfront was taken in the early 1900s. The schooner has its decks loaded with lumber and men standing on the lumber, making ready to leave for a distant port. It is docked in the part of Liverpool now used primarily as a parking lot, though there are dreams of making it a vibrant part of the town once more. The Liverpool Town Hall, built in 1902, can be seen in the background

The picture was taken from the bridge crossing the harbour; when the ship was ready to sail out, a span of the bridge would be cranked open with a special key, now in the collection of the Queens County Museum, so that the vessel could leave. Gilbert Kempton Jr., son of the Liverpool photographer Gilbert Kempton, could remember having a "good many rides on the turntable bridge when it was opened and shut to allow vessels to go up the river, some as far as Milton, to load lumber." Ships could sail to the tidewater mark on the Mersey River, and if that could be done today, Liverpool and Milton would have a priceless yachting and recreation area.

LIVERPOOL WATER-FRONT, 1906

This 1906 photograph shows the waterfront in Liverpool with the post office clock tower in the centre background. At one point the waterfront defined Liverpool's existence. Not only did privateering and trade make many Liverpool families wealthy, but the waterfront was the scene of a flourishing shipbuilding industry. Fishing, the number one export from Liverpool until the middle of the nineteenth century, was carried on by Liverpool fishing vessels, and when lumber became the main export from the town, it left on the ships shown above. When the United States imposed prohibition after World War One, the harbour became a centre for the rum-running trade. Author Thomas H. Raddall notes in his autobiography, "every time I passed over the river bridge at Liverpool I could see rum-running craft of all kinds refitting, fuelling and victualling for the next voyage." Rum-running voyages took a triangular route from Liverpool to St. Pierre, off Newfoundland, then to the coast of the United States.

LIVERPOOL STREET SCENE, 1891
TOP RIGHT

This fine old photograph gives a good sense of the flavour of downtown life in Liverpool in the last decade of the nineteenth century. It was taken in 1891, just four years before all of the businesses seen in the picture were destroyed in the great Liverpool fire of 1895, which consumed more than sixty buildings. Among the businesses which can be seen, looking left to right, are George Snaddon's store on the corner, which sold china, glass, crockery, and furniture and burned three times before Snaddon gave the business up and retired; Thomas Bird, jeweller; D.C. Mulhall, groceries; A.W. Hendry, groceries; N.S. Wetmore, jewellery store; and the London Fruit Store.

LOOKING WEST FROM SIMEON PERKINS' HOUSE, C.1890
BOTTOM RIGHT

The young girls in this picture were children and teenagers over a century ago when they stood facing the photographer outside the fence of what today is Simeon Perkins' house and the Queens County Museum in Liverpool. We know from faded information on the back of the photograph that the one on the far left was a Sterns, her first name unintelligible. Alice Albro was the child next to her, then came Mary Patch, Gladys Freeman, and Lizzie Sterns. From records in the museum we know that Mary Patch was born in 1875, lived in a grand house on Liverpool's Main Street and died in 1972; that Alice Albro married Riger Aitken in Quebec on June 11, 1901; and that Lizzie Sterns, daughter of Heber Sterns, married an Englishman, William Sidley, in Panama in 1910.

LIVERPOOL STREET SCENE, 1891

LOOKING WEST FROM SIMEON PERKINS' HOUSE, C.1890

THE SOUTH END OF MAIN STREET, LIVERPOOL, C.1907

This postcard was sent from Liverpool to California on August 29, 1907. On the back, it says: "This scene is just a little way from us, taken from the opposite corner of the block we live in. The street leads right down to the lighthouse at Fort Point …One of my cousins lives opposite the white house that stands out on the right hand side. This morning I got up early and took a walk to College Hill, the site of a college that was burned years ago. It gives a fine view of the whole town only now there are so many trees in leaf that you can't see the houses …I picked some wild flowers I'd like to send you. Think of picking buttercups the last of August. Not so many wild flowers here as down in Maine, nor such pretty ones but cultivated ones do much better. Nature seems to make it up to the Maine people for what they cannot raise."

THE ROYAL BANK, BUILT IN 1914-15 ON THE SITE OF SNADDON'S STORE, C.1920S

This former Royal Bank building was opened in 1915 on the site of three versions of Snaddon's Store, each of which burned, the last in the fire of 1914. In February 1915, Caledonia's *The Gold Hunter* reported that the new bank was housed in a fine building built of reinforced concrete with the front of face brick and terra cotta, with a granite base. The newspaper said that "the first floor is occupied solely by the bank, and the splendid banking room is finished in quartered oak, with Tennessee marble base, the walls being burlapped." In building the bank, preference had been given to local industries and labour, with the woodwork handled by Walker Brothers of Milton, plumbing and heating by Charles Wigglesworth, and painting by E.C. Hagen. "The work is very creditable and satisfactory," the newspaper reported.

The manager was proud of the new structure saying, "we have a staff of seven to man the howitzers," the suggestion being, according to the newspaper, "that this institution is a veritable fortress sufficiently strong to repel all attacks by an enemy, and protect depositors' money, while all peaceful citizens are treated with respect, and their patronage cordially invited." In 1989, after a great deal of research by the community and bank officials, the bank built a reproduction of a house erected in the 1850s by Benjamin DeWolfe and moved its operations there. The old building became, among other things, a pizza parlour.

INDIAN GARDENS, ONCE A MAJOR MI'KMAQ GATHERING PLACE, C.1930S

Below Lake Rossignol and just above Milton was an area which came to be known as Indian Gardens, a place traditionally used by the Mi'kmaq as a gathering area and encampment. Author Thomas H. Raddall found many Mi'kmaq artifacts in the area and thought that the Mi'kmaq occupied it in some numbers to the mid-1700s. He believed that some disaster, such as an infectious disease, typhus or scurvy, decimated the population there.

Raddall married in 1927. He and his bride Edith Freeman spent their honeymoon at Indian Gardens, trout fishing and enjoying both the sunshine and moonshine of early summer. But it was a paradise soon to be lost. A power dam was constructed below the gardens in 1928, washing out "a vast scatter of stone tools, arrowheads, bits of pottery and other primitive artifacts." He lamented the lost beauty of the area and said that the gardens now lay "under about seventy feet of water, and the site of our honeymoon lies drowned and buried with them." This photograph was taken in the Indian Gardens area by Will Thorpe.

BRIDGE AT MILTON SHOWING THE RAPIDS, C.1908

The village of Milton lies along both sides of the Mersey River, just above Liverpool. It was settled immediately after the establishment of Liverpool, since the falls on the river presented an opportunity to set up lumber mills. In fact, for the first years of its existence Milton was called The Falls. Since the community was strung along both sides of the river there quickly grew a demand for bridges to connect it, and over the years there have been a number of different bridges to carry out that role. In Simeon Perkins' diary there is mention of the construction of the Great Bridge at The Falls in 1791, a bridge destroyed by a tidal wave in 1813. The bridge shown in this photograph was constructed in 1900, the iron for the bridge manufactured in New Glasgow, Nova Scotia.

The second photograph shows the view from the east end of the bridge, with Alister Harlow's photography studio on the upper floor of the first building on the right. It is assumed that Alister Harlow took these photographs. Both are from the collection in the Queens County Museum and were donated to the museum by Tim McDonald.

MAIN STREET, MILTON, C.1910

There were always great hopes for Milton. Samuel Hunt, writing in 1860, predicted that one day Milton would become as handsome a little inland town as any in the province. He said "there will be back streets laid out on the Eastern and the Western side of Milton River, and roads leading from the main road to them, which will afford their sons to settle on the land of their birth." James More's history, published thirteen years later, said that Milton had steadily increased in population and wealth, and that many of the leading merchants in the county did business there. "There are now five places of public worship in the village, and a handsome Academy on the west side of the river. The merchants and others have lately established a reading room which reflects a great credit upon them, and from which they may glean not only the passing news of their community but that of the world, for upon its table are to be found the leading English, American and Canadian journals and magazines. The building of a railroad across the country, and the consequent opening up of the interior will largely benefit Milton, and increase its facilities for becoming a large manufacturing centre."

One of the newspapers, *The Advance* (Liverpool), had already been enthusiastic. In 1855 it wrote that Milton and Liverpool would one day combine. "The probability is," the newspaper said, "if circumstances continue to make progress as at present, that the village and town will, ere many years elapse, be connected, and form a second Nova Scotia City." Today, Milton and Liverpool have in many senses come together—the village ends where Liverpool begins, and politically the entire county is united in the Region of Queens—but the predicted growth and prosperity did not materialize to its fullest extent. Milton remains, however, a good place to live, with lovely old homes and beautiful vistas along the Mersey.

THE BOOMING SEAPORT OF PORT MEDWAY, 1894

If Liverpool was one of the most important ports for shipping in Maritime Canada during the mid 1800s, Port Medway was not far behind. It was involved in fishing, shipping lumber, privateering and shipbuilding—Marguerite Letson's history of Port Medway lists 150 ships built in the port between 1808 and 1900. Said Letson: "Sailors thronged in the busy streets, taverns were plenty, but withal, there was little disorder for the leaders of the town had a strong sense of civic responsibility, and a tradition of deep-sea discipline."

The town was even large enough to have two school districts, with two school houses erected prior to 1840. When the two schools were combined, one of the older buildings became the home of the Sons of Temperance, organized in 1862 to combat drunkenness brought to the area by sailors involved in the West Indies trade. These two photographs show a view of Port Medway looking toward the harbour and the Port Medway post office.

THE POST OFFICE AT PORT MEDWAY, C.1905

MILL VILLAGE, 1890

Mill Village, upriver from Port Medway on the Medway River, was also known as Mills Village and Port Mills. It received its name from sawmills and grist mills which were established there in the 1760s, making them among the earliest mills in the county. In this photograph a little girl dressed in her best sits on a log across the river from the waterwheel-powered mill, owned by E.D. Davison. This photograph was taken from the bridge in front of the house owned by Dr. Freeman Smith, a Mill Village medical doctor and grandson of Josiah Smith, one of the first settlers in the Northern District. The original is in the Yarmouth County Museum. It was taken on November 16, 1890, by Bridgewater photographer Aaron Rhodes, who carried out photographic assignments for E.D. Davison.

MILL VILLAGE FROM THE BRIDGE, C.1905

BOTTOM RIGHT

This picture was made into a popular postcard, one which has turned up in a number of collections. The buildings shown in the photograph are, from left to right, the Methodist Meeting house, built in 1898; the Mill Village school, built in 1865; George Hatt's Little Shop; the Baptist Meeting House, opened in 1859; Steadman's Factory and Steadman's house.

The schoolhouse in this picture was described in the provincial report on education for 1865 as a fine school, costing upwards of $1200. It "was built in this section during the last summer, and is now, I believe, ready for occupation," the inspector wrote. The school was part of a construction boom in public schools which took place at this time. In 1865 alone 164 new schools were built in Nova Scotia, 136 were in the process of being built and 520 were being planned. The inspector said it marked the beginning of an era in provincial history, "unparalleled in our annals."

THE MEDWAY RIVER, RUNNING THROUGH MILL VILLAGE, C.1900S

R.R. McLeod, who wrote extensively about the history of Queens County at the end of the nineteenth century, said of Mill Village that no one expected to ever see a city where the village now stood, "but it will always have the charm of a beautiful river in its midst, and many other delightful features. Not the least of attractions," he said, "is the noted salmon fishing, that begins early and lasts a long time." McLeod said that the village had been founded by people who had been attracted by "opportunities for procuring large quantities of fine pine timber and good mill sites," which were "inducements enough to attract energetic men who did not stick at trifles."

MILL VILLAGE FROM THE BRIDGE, C.1905

BROOKLYN AS SEEN FROM LIVERPOOL, C.1906

Brooklyn was first of all a camping area for the Mi'kmaq and then, in the 1630s, the site of an attempt by Nicholas Denys and Isaac de Razilly to establish a fishery. That failed to last, however, and it wasn't until the arrival of the settlers from New England that permanent settlement was successful. At one time it was called Herring Cove, and in the mid-1850s the harbour of Herring Cover was said to hold twenty sail at all times in safety. Today the area is home to the Brooklyn Marina and the harbour is filled both with pleasure craft and with vessels coming in to load newsprint from the Bowater Mersey Paper Company plant, which opened in 1929.

A FISHERMAN'S HOME AT EAST PORT L'HEBERT, C.1900S

PHOTOS AT RIGHT

This lovely seaside house still sits by the shores of Port L'Hebert Bay. At one time it was the home of James and Annie Tupper, just down the coast from the Port L'Hebert lighthouse on Shingle Point. James Tupper used the boat on the shore to go out into the bay to haul lobster traps and fish, sometimes offloading the catch into a wagon pulled by an ox down into the water. Today, near the house, there is a concrete government wharf used by many different fishing boats. James was born in Port Medway, moved to East Side Port L'Hebert when he was eight and died in 1956 at the age of 85. He married Annie Wolfe in 1897; she died in 1958 at the age of 84. These photographs of the exterior and the parlour of the Tupper house are in the possession of Mrs. Marilyn Clarke of East Port L'Hebert, who used to live in the house when she helped care for James and Annie Tupper in their old age. Annie Tupper was Marilyn Clarke's great-aunt.

A FISHERMAN'S HOME AT EAST PORT L'HEBERT, C.1900S

FISHERMAN'S HOME, INTERIOR VIEW

THE ENTRANCE TO PORT MOUTON, 1939

A traveller entering Port Mouton from the east would see a similar scene today, though the railway tracks have gone. The French carried on a fishery in the area for 150 years, and, at the same time as the New England settlers founded Liverpool, in 1759, fishermen were establishing a settlement at Port Mouton. There were no roads, of course, with homes being built along the shore.

The name Port Mouton came about when Sieur De Monts sailed to the area in 1604 to investigate suitable locations for fishing and fur trading. He put into a harbour west of what was to become Liverpool, staying there a month. During that time a sheep was lost overboard, giving the name Port Mouton to the area. Different names were tried out—at one point it was called Lebanon and at another Guysborough—but the name Port Mouton stuck. Settlement began in earnest after the American Revolutionary War ended in 1783, when a number of disbanded soldiers under the command of Sir Guy Carleton settled there. After a destructive fire, however, they left and reestablished themselves in what is now known as Guysborough County, named after the commander.

PORT MOUTON, SHOWING ITS FAMOUS ROUND BUILDING, C.1904

This building was constructed around 1900, according to Queens County historian Armand Wigglesworth. He says it was originally a temperance building—the movement was at one time very strong in Queens County—and that it was not actually round, but octagonal in shape. It was the most unique building of its day. The Oddfellows occupied the upper storey at first, and later the hall served as a community centre for meetings, socials, pie sales, and dances. Wigglesworth said the design was the inspiration of a Liverpool carpenter who felt that a different kind of design could be used as a novelty. Wigglesworth said, "His proposal was accepted and as a result the building became a well-known landmark." It stood in central Port Mouton and was also used for a time as a school, while the Port Mouton Consolidated school was being built in 1960-61. The building fell into disrepair soon after, however, and in 1969 it was torn down. The photograph was taken from the journal *Acadiensis*, published in 1904.

THE WHITE SANDS OF SUMMERVILLE BEACH, C.1920S AND 1940S

One of the finest white sand beaches in the Atlantic Provinces is located at Summerville Beach, about fifteen kilometres southwest of Liverpool. Over the years, it has been a centre of leisure activities for the people of Liverpool and surrounding areas and has always attracted the tourist trade. These photographs, taken during two different decades, show swimmers and cottages.

According to a 1939 Summerville advertisement, cottages were available weekly or overnight for picnic parties, and a verandah was available for private dance parties. The earliest name for Summerville Beach was Flat Rocks but the new name was more conducive to the tourist industry, one of the mainstays of the local economy. In the mid-1800s large amounts of the white sands of Summerville Beach were sold each year to places like Halifax, a practice which is today forbidden.

THE FIRST FRAMED HOUSE IN THE NORTHERN DISTRICT, C.1890S

This photograph shows, attached to the right of the house and behind the wagon, the parlour of the first framed house in the Northern District. It was built in South Brookfield by Captain Josiah Smith, the son of Stephen Smith, one of the original settlers of Liverpool. After a life at sea, Captain Smith moved his wife and family inland, in 1813, bought the log cabin owned by William Burke, the first settler in the Northern District, and established a farm, which exists today. He also established the first store in the area and set up both a sawmill and a grist mill. Burke, for his part, moved to a nearby location.

Josiah Smith's daughter Ann was the mother of Robert Randall McLeod, the noted writer and naturalist. Of his grandfather Smith, McLeod wrote in his 1912 history of the Northern District that "my mother was his daughter, and rode behind him on horseback when a very little girl, as she made her first trip into the country." The Smith property is today a lovely place on the river and is occupied by Mrs. Freda Smith, widow of Dr. Harry Smith, who carried on a medical practice in North Queens from 1938 until his death in 1964. Dr. Smith was the son of Samuel Primrose Smith and the great-grandson of Captain Josiah Smith. The photograph, in the Kejimkujik National Park collection, is used with the permission of Mrs. Freda Smith.

MOOSE HARBOUR AND WESTERN HEAD, NEAR THE MOUTH OF LIVERPOOL BAY, 1909

This photograph, taken from a postcard in the Provincial Archives, shows Western Head in the early years of the twentieth century. Situated on a headland on the western side of the bay leading in to Liverpool, it began in the 1820s as a settlement established by Germans from Lunenburg. The author Thomas H. Raddall had a cabin in adjacent Moose Harbour where he sometimes wrote. In his diary entry for May 22, 1955, Raddall noted that the weather was very hot and that a brush fire had sprung up. His wife had a picnic prepared to take out to the cabin but Raddall worried about the fire. As he recounts in his memoirs, he drove alone towards his cabin but was turned back by police, dense smoke covering everything. As it turned out, the fire destroyed his cabin, as well as fishing boats, houses, cottages, the school in Mersey Point and more. "Had we been there on our picnic," Raddall said in his diary, "we'd have had to jump into the sea." The day before he had been working in his cabin on the manuscript for his novel *The Wings of Night* but for some unaccountable and lucky reason, he had taken it home with him that night.

THE CORNER AT SOUTH BROOKFIELD, IN THE 1890S AND 1900S

PHOTOS AT RIGHT

These two photographs show the first settled area in the Northern District. William Burke built his cabin not far from this corner and author R.R. McLeod's home was the house at the top of the older photograph. Today the intersection in the picture—the spot at which one either goes to Liverpool or Bridgewater—is widened and paved. There are no businesses there, just a post office and homes sitting beside the Medway River and along the highway. When these pictures, provided by Beryl Berringer, were taken, there were or had been inns, tanneries, blacksmith shops, wagon makers' shops, sawmills, a shingle mill, carding mills, a shoemaker's shop, brick kiln, restaurants, and stores in the community. South Brookfield had even had its own conflagration, a fire in 1864 that burned most of the buildings clustered around the corner.

Two views of the corner at South Brookfield, in the 1890s and 1900s

THE HISTORY OF A VILLAGE IN A PHOTOGRAPH, CALEDONIA C.1909

This picture, taken from the steeple of the United Church in Caledonia, tells much about the village. At the top of the photograph in the centre is the rounded roof of the Masonic Hall, built between 1890 and 1892 in the same style as Liverpool's early Masonic Hall. Just below that is the N.F. Douglas store, built to replace an earlier store in 1907. On this side of the store is the entrance to the old West Caledonia Road, and then there is the Alton House, built in 1860 and run for years as a hotel. The building across the driveway from the Alton House and at the edge of the road was what historian Leone Smith described as a combined store and dwelling belonging to Brenton Harlow, who lived upstairs with his wife Dorothy, the daughter of *The Gold Hunter* newspaper editor W.H. Banks. The buildings across the street housed a harness shop and barber shop. The building in the lower left foreground, whose top can just be seen, was W.H. Banks' printing office between 1906 and 1910. For a time, the newspaper offices were located in a building to the north of the Baptist Church, but in 1910 this building was moved to that spot, where it continued as the newspaper building until it burned in October, 1941. The earlier building can be seen in a photograph in chapter five.

TWO ICE CREAM PARLOURS AND A BANK, CALEDONIA, 1928

In this photograph, taken from a spot near the current United Church and looking toward the Caledonia corner, two ice cream parlours and the community's first bank can be seen. Ice cream parlours were popular in the 1920s and 1930s. The one on the left was located in a shop that used to stand near the road in front of both the Jonas Parker house, built in 1850, and the Alton House hotel. The building was used both as a dwelling and a shop. The ice cream parlour was begun by John G. Shirreffs of Whiteburn but was moved to make way for the post office, opened in 1959.

The ice cream parlour across the street was owned by Mrs. Philson Wamboldt. Prior to that it had been used, according to Leone Smith's *The History of Caledonia*, as a confectionary store and a restaurant. As for the bank, the area's board of trade began agitating for a bank in 1911. The story was that the Bank of Nova Scotia made the decision to open a branch after *The Gold Hunter* published a false story suggesting that another bank was coming to the community. The bank was opened on the fourth of March, 1919, operating there until a new brick bank building was constructed beside the N.F. Douglas General Store in 1931. That bank continued until March of 2001, when the Bank of Nova Scotia, in part of a program to close down banks in rural communities, closed its doors.

POST OFFICE AND RESIDENCE OF D.F. MCADAM, CALEDONIA, C.1910

The home shown in this photograph is near the present post office, just south of the Caledonia corner. Leone Smith records that it was built around 1896 by Dan McAdam. The contract Mr. McAdam had as postmaster in Caledonia was dated 1898 to 1918. "Mr. McAdam," wrote Leone Smith, "passed away before his contract was fulfilled, and his wife May finished out his term. Then Mrs. McAdam had a contract for five years 1929-1925." Mr. and Mrs. Dan McAdam had two daughters, Gladys and Bessie.

Smith went on to say that Clarke Murray bought the home and post office and continued as postmaster from 1926 until 1956, at which time his wife Beulah carried on as postmistress until Pearl Delong took over the position. Delong was postmaster at Caledonia when the current post office building was opened in June of 1959. The first postal way station had been opened in Caledonia in 1855, on the site of the Alton House hotel, which was just two buildings to the north of the present post office.

The photograph of the McAdam house was taken from a 1910 postcard sent to Mrs. A.A. Whitman, in Torbrook, Annapolis County. On the back it says: "Dear Mrs. Whitman, Reached home safely but oh so tired! We drove to the 'falls' when we found the train was so late. I never had a better time in my life than those 3 days. Love to all the folks. Write me a long letter soon. Lovingly, Lulu."

TELEPHONE SERVICE IN THE NORTHERN DISTRICT, C.1960S

In the late 1880s, gold mining brought the first telephones to North Queens, made possible by private mining company lines connected through Bridgewater. Regular telephone service in Caledonia began in 1904, the first operator being Mrs. Byron Kempton, wife of the owner of Alton House, where the exchange was located. By 1910 the telephone directory for the Northern District listed eleven telephones for Caledonia, which included three doctors, the N.F. Douglas store, the Alton House, the Commercial House, and the railway station; three telephones in Harmony, including the pulp mill; two in Kempt; three in Maitland Bridge; and four for South Brookfield, including one at Pinehurst, the lodge overlooking the Christopher Lakes.

The old switching system, manned in the above photograph by Edna MacKay, left, and Bessie Douglas, right, was in operation as late as 1973, when it became automated. Community members missed the informality of the old system. If a caller were looking for someone who was not at home, the operators would often say where the person was visiting and make the connection with the missing party. This photograph was made available by Eugene Penney, in whose house the switching system was located.

Bridge at Greenfield N.S.

BRIDGE OVER THE MEDWAY RIVER, GREENFIELD C.1908

Greebfield is one of the prettiest parts of Queens County and has long been a prime recreational area. The Medway River, which flows out of Ponhook Lake, runs through Greenfield, Charleston, Mill Village, and finally Port Medway, on its way to the ocean. From the moment settlers began settling the Greenfield area there were demands for bridges across the river. The first bridge across the Medway lost its footings each year as the ice came out of Ponhook Lake, until the bridge built in 1900 used iron guards to protect the piers. This photograph shows that bridge. It was largely wooden and was replaced by an iron bridge in 1914, which lasted until the current bridge was built.

THE VILLAGE OF KEMPT, WITH ITS GENERAL STORE, C.1920S, AND SERVICE STATION, C.1930S

PHOTOS AT RIGHT

The village of Kempt has changed only slightly since these photographs were taken seventy and eighty years ago. Oickle's Service Station has been replaced by Wilfred Ringer's Service Station, the last refuelling stop for visitors on their way to Kejimkujik National Park. It is in the same location as the service station in this picture, though the house next to the station is gone. The store in the earlier photograph is across from the service station and later was the home of one of the area's best-loved citizens, Jordan Anthony, who died in 2001 at the age of ninety-six. The store was run by Humphrey DeLong, who was born in 1886 and who died in 1943. The man on the wagon is John Henry Lewis, of New Grafton, who was born in 1866 and who died in 1943.

Lieutenant-Governor Sir James Kempt visited the area in 1822, a visit for which the village is named, though coincidentally it was founded by Francis, Richard, and Thomas Kempton. A Baptist church was built in the village in the 1850s and was replaced with another in 1904. Today the village is known far and wide for its strawberry and harvest suppers, which have been held for over fifty years, the strawberries used in the early years being wild. The first was held by Jordan Anthony and his wife, Betty, on their farm in nearby Northfield.

DELONG'S STORE IN KEMPT, C.1920S

OICKLE'S SERVICE STATION AT KEMPT, C.1930S

ON THE BEAUTIFUL ROSETTE ROAD, NEAR WESTFIELD, C.1910S

The home in this photograph is located about as close to paradise as you can get in the material world. It is situated on the Rosette Road, which winds from North Brookfield to Westfield, sitting on lush ground between two lakes. The original part of the house was built between 1820 and 1840 by James Daley, the son of the original James Daley who followed William Burke into the Northern District in 1801. The first James Daley had another son named Wentworth, the first baby born to settlers in the Northern District. The house is lived in today by Judy, great-great-granddaughter of the James who built the house, and Eric Cole.

There was a mill on the property almost from the beginning, one which operated for close to a hundred years. It was the lumber from the Daley mill which was used to build the first houses in Caledonia. In 1884 James Slocum Dailey—the name gradually came to be spelled with an "i"—constructed the old mill, timing his enterprise nicely with the discovery of gold in the Northern District. Before long the mill was frantically turning out lumber, timbers, planking, shingles, fence pickets and laths, providing employment to men from all over the area. It operated something akin to a modern building supply company, ordering in supplies for people in the surrounding area. In the 1930s the mill was sold to the Nova Scotia Woodenware owners in South Brookfield. The picture was provided by Judy Cole.

Chapter 2

Landmarks Past and Present

HISTORIC HOMES AND IMPORTANT BUILDINGS

THE SELDON HOUSE, LIVERPOOL, C.1910

The beautiful house in this photograph, shown with its terraced lawns, still stands in Liverpool, but it is sometimes difficult to pick out. The lawns are gone, covered by another house built where they used to stand. The house itself has been changed and now has artificial siding. A school once stood on the site, giving the name of School Street to the street running up the hill beside the house. The house was built in the early 1900s by John F. Seldon, who named it Hillcrest. A pen and ink sketch of the house appeared in the newspaper after it was completed in 1908. John Seldon died in 1930. In 1928 the property was purchased by the Mersey Paper Company as the home of its president, Colonel C.H.L. Jones. When Jones died the property was bought by Alton and Elise Snow, who converted it into a hotel known as the Hillcrest Inn.

SIMEON PERKINS HOUSE, LIVERPOOL, BUILT 1767, PHOTOS C.1936 AND 1960s

The most storied house in all of Queens County is that of Simeon Perkins, whose house now anchors the Queens County Museum. Simeon Perkins built the house over 1766 and 1767—on March 26, 1767 he noted in his famous diary that "the house is not ready, no glass"—and built it in a style with which he was familiar. Allen Penney, who prepared a curatorial report on Perkins House for the Nova Scotia Museum, called the style "New England." Penney didn't like to call the house a Cape Cod house, observing that it was built in a uniquely North American style used from South Carolina to Nova Scotia during the mid-1800s, a style which had been developed from Medieval English houses.

Simeon Perkins arrived in Liverpool from Connecticut in 1762, three years after it had been founded by settlers also from New England. Although free grants of land had been made to the first settlers, there were none left for him. The town proprietors drew up a series of lots close to the harbour entrance to accommodate those who were looking for land, allowing Perkins to draw lot B3, which was a good size in relation to the others. The area was isolated at first, but soon the town grew out to embrace his land. In building the house, he made use of materials available from the surrounding area, though the bricks and hardware were likely imported. Large trees were squared in the forest for framing, with lumber milled at The Falls (Milton) for boarding in. The house was expanded in 1781 with an addition put on the left side of the house and again in 1792, when a new kitchen was added at the back.

Perkins lived mainly in this house, though he did have two other houses—one near his mills at The Falls. Only one other family occupied the house before it was acquired by the Queens County Historical Society. Allen Penney sums up the effect of the house nicely when he says that it "may be interpreted as modest while exhibiting an awareness of social status, sophistication and prestige, all of which were firmly established in the mind of a young merchant of thirty-one years of age at the time of its building." In 1959, largely due to the efforts of acclaimed author and historian Thomas H. Raddall, who was head of the historical society at the time, Simeon Perkins House was opened as the first of the historical houses belonging to the Nova Scotia Museum.

The 1960s photograph above is credited to the Nova Scotia Communications and Information Centre and is courtesy of the Queens County Museum. The older photo on page 32 is courtesy of the Nova Scotia Archives and Records Management.

SYLVANUS COBB'S HOUSE IN LIVERPOOL, BUILT IN THE 1760S, C.1900

Built at the time the township was founded, the house shown in this photograph was for many years the oldest in Liverpool. It was described as being in an excellent state of preservation as late as 1936, but it was gone by 1945, having fallen prey to two fires. It was built by Sylvanus Cobb, one of the earliest of the privateer captains and said to have held letters of marque against the French in 1744. Cobb captained the ship used by General James Wolfe in the siege of Louisburg, and was one of the proprietors who selected the site of the future township of Liverpool. He built his house in Liverpool as soon as the settlers arrived and planned to carry on business in Liverpool, having applied for land on which to build a store and wharf, but he died in 1762.

Sylvanus Cobb built his house from materials he brought from New England. The local newspaper said that firemen had been called out in January of 1942 to try to save the house but that it was ruined beyond repair, the old New England red pine burning rapidly. The shell of the house was saved, but in November of 1945, firemen were called out again. Vagrants had built a fire on the floor of the old house, setting it ablaze. Firemen found the house a raging inferno and were helpless as it burned to the ground. "The first house built in Liverpool and the oldest inhabited house in Eastern Canada," said *The Advance*, "has passed from view."

DEXTER'S TAVERN, DATING FROM THE FOUNDING OF LIVERPOOL, C.1950s

This photograph, taken by E.G.L. Wetmore and found in the Public Archives, shows the oldest structure in Liverpool. In the first years of the town it existed as Dexter's Tavern, near Fort Point, to serve the soldiers stationed there. As well, the ferry service from Herring Cove, later called Brooklyn, landed at the tavern. It was an ideal site; materials to build it were found near by. The timbers were hand hewn and the nails hand forged. It was originally put up as a home by Daniel Eldridge but when he ran into financial difficulties it was bought at auction by Enoch Dexter, who ran it as a tavern.

According to *Some Liverpool Chronicles*, practically all public business was carried on in the taverns. "These were private houses whose owners, known as tavern keepers, were licensed to provide liquor, food and lodging at established prices." Simeon Perkins often mentions Dexter's Tavern, as in his entry for May 28, 1772, when he records that "the owners of the schooner *Betsey*, lately purchased by Capt. John Cobb, met at Dexter's to settle amount." It is said that the massive stones used in the foundation of the building came from Fortress Louisburg. Enoch Dexter's widow Mary Dexter carried on her husband's business, but when she died the building became a private dwelling, which it still is today.

THE COURT HOUSE, LIVERPOOL, C.1909

Built in 1854, the Court House was described in *South Shore; Seasoned Timbers* as perhaps the finest expression in the province of the American Greek Revival Movement, which spread north, west, and south from Philadelphia, New York and Boston in the years between 1820 and 1860. The authorities in Liverpool had requested a "plain, good and substantial courthouse" and the plans were drawn up by a Liverpool carpenter, William G. Hammond. It was built by George W. Boehner, originally from Liverpool, who was only twenty-six at the time. A feature of the court house is the series of fluted Doric columns at the front. In 1969, renovations lowered the ceiling in the courtroom and saw the exterior painted white. Further renovations occurred in 1999, with repairs to both the interior and the exterior of the building. The replaced columns and windows, which could not be saved, were turned over to the Mersey Heritage Society. In July 2001 the Court House was declared a Provincial Heritage Property. The photograph was taken by Liverpool photographer Gilbert Kempton and is used with permission of the Queens County Museum.

THE TOWN HALL, LIVERPOOL, C. 1910

Liverpool's Town Hall, shown in this photograph in 1910, was designated a National Historic Site in 1989. The designation describes it as one of the most impressive completely wooden municipal buildings of its size and style found anywhere in Canada. It was constructed over 1901 and 1902 and contained not only town government offices, but an opera house seating over 400 downstairs and another 150 in the balcony. Today the building houses the Sherman Hines Photography Museum, while the opera house is the Astor Theatre, site of the Liverpool International Theatre Festival, dramatic productions put on by the Winds of Change amateur theatre group, and films.

The Town Hall cost $12,500 to build. It was designed by Halifax architect Herbert Gates and constructed by A.H. Boucher, who was responsible for many of the buildings in Queens County. *The Advance* and *Western Counties Advocate* remarks that when nearing completion, the Town Hall was "up to date in every respect, and provided with all modern fittings and conveniences, and its admirable situation at the junction of Main and Gorham Streets, serves to set off to the best advantage the work of the architect. The style—the old colonial—fits in not at all badly with the general effect of surrounding buildings." The newspaper went on to say that the ground floor of the building was devoted to offices, including those of the town clerk and treasurer, a court room, a police office, a reading room, and rooms for a registry of deeds and a probate office.

The newspaper reported that upstairs in the new building there was a large assembly room which could be used for dances, banquets, sociables, tea-meetings, or other similar purposes, plus a council chamber, which was described as "a fine room with cloak and toilet rooms annexed." Floors in the building were made of black birch and the rest of cypress, according to *The Advance*. The opera house was finished "in embossed metal with panels and mouldings in bold relief, lighted by an electrolier carrying 37 lights of 32 candle power, and by a number of bracket lights from the walls, there being also three rows of foot-lights." The town offices moved out of the building in 1996, when the town and county amalgamated in one regional government.

LANDMARKS PAST AND PRESENT

Two Liverpool hotels:

The Trilby, c.1880, and the Thorndike, c.1895

Over the years, Liverpool has had an unusual number of hotels. The port of Liverpool was a busy place during the age of sail, with ships constantly coming in and out of the harbour. People disembarking from the various vessels needed places to stay and enterprising local inhabitants provided accommodations. Three of the many hotels were in the same location over the years, each replacing the one before when it was destroyed by fire. The pictures on this page show the Trilby Hotel, above, on the corner of Main and Court streets, and the Thorndike Hotel, below, which replaced it. Much like modern hotels, the Trilby set aside the ground floor for stores and businesses and located the hotel on the second and third floors. Its picture is courtesy of Tim McDonald, who was given the rare photograph years after it was found floating in the Mersey River. The Thorndike, whose photograph is courtesy of the Queens County Museum, also devoted the first floor to stores and businesses and the second and third to guests. It burned in 1902. The next hotel to occupy the space was the Mersey, which still exists today. It is now a block of apartments.

38 HISTORIC QUEENS COUNTY

THE MERSEY HOTEL, C.1910S

On December 21, 1904, *The Advance* reported with satisfaction that work on building the new Mersey Hotel was almost finished and that the furniture was being installed. "It certainly is a most handsome and valuable addition to the town, and its opening, just as the railway has come, is to be regarded as particularly opportune." The hotel opened on New Year's Day, 1905. Designed by a Halifax architect, the hotel was built by Boehner Brothers of LaHave. Boehner Brothers had been started by George W. Boehner of Liverpool, who had built the Liverpool Court House in 1854. The newspapers noted that the Mersey Hotel had a dining room that seated seventy-five people comfortably and that the building was heated by a thorough system of hot water radiators. The first floor also contained offices, a writing room with four desks and a large table, three sample rooms, lavatories, a kitchen with a large range and a charcoal broiler, pantry, and laundry. The second floor contained a parlour, an apartment, a waiting room, and "fourteen roomy sleeping apartments." The parlour and waiting room opened onto the verandah through French doors. On the third floor were nineteen bedrooms, and "those matrimonially inclined will hear with satisfaction that the house is equipped with two handsome bridal chambers."

Advertisements for the hotel described it as splendidly furnished throughout and equipped with every modern convenience, including electric lights and telephones in every room. It had one of the finest dining rooms in the province and was "within one hour's drive of the finest salmon fishing, duck shooting and moose hunting region in Nova Scotia."

The Elmwood Hotel, c.1920 and the International Hotel, c.1890

The Elmwood Hotel, top left, stood on the property in front of Simeon Perkins House, on land which is now a part of the grounds of the Queens County Museum. It was opened in 1915 in the John H. Freeman house by C. Gordon Jones, who advertised in the press that everything would be home-like about the establishment. "The living room, the large smoking-room, the dining room, with its many tables to accommodate just four persons each, the open hearths, are all fully up-to-date, while the bedrooms are airy and spacious." During World War Two the Elmwood was used by the Canadian Navy for officers' quarters, with a drill hall built behind it. Armand Wigglesworth wrote in the newspaper that he could remember the hotel as a cosy, comfy place "which came to a sad end." After a cold winter, with no heat in the building, the pipes froze and flooded the old hotel. It, along with the drill hall, was torn down.

J.W. Cobb was the proprietor of the International Hotel, at bottom, which was set back under the shade of trees, with chairs on the verandah for guests. This photograph was taken around 1890. An advertisement dated October 8, 1886 in *The Caledonia Times* said that the house was pleasantly situated in the centre of town. "The rooms are large and pleasant and furnished with all the modern conveniences. The premises are close to the livery of A.L. West, and the Northern and Western coaches pass the door daily." The new Town Hall was built on the site of this hotel in 1902. Across the street was the store of F.L. Seldon, which sold groceries, flour, and feed.

THE ELMWOOD HOTEL,
TOP RIGHT

THE INTERNATIONAL HOTEL,
BOTTOM RIGHT

THE LIVERPOOL POST OFFICE, 1904

When one drives into Liverpool today, a plain brick federal building greets those who have need of a post office. For some unaccountable reason, a number of Nova Scotia towns—Wolfville is another—lost historic and beautiful brick and stone buildings when old post offices were destroyed and modern buildings put in their place. The arguments for such demolition ranged from the condition of the buildings to the economics of maintaining them, but the result was the same: towns lost landmark buildings.

The post office shown in this photograph, sporting a beautiful clock tower and at one time covered with ivy, was built in 1898. It was demolished in 1955, and as one account of the time said, "The contractors are already starting to make plans to tear down the old post office in Liverpool, and soon the finest building in Liverpool will be only a memory." The cornerstone for the new building, described in news reports as being functional and ugly, as well as being out of keeping with the older architecture in Liverpool, was laid by Senator Donald Smith on September 12, 1955.

At one time, the people of Liverpool would not put up with a post office that was not beautiful as well as functional. An editorial in *The Advance* of April 1898 applauded the fact that work was about to begin on the new post office, but said that while utility was no doubt the most important thing to consider, the question of appearance was entitled to due weight. "Such a building should contribute to the beauty and attractiveness of the town."

The arches in the picture were to celebrate Dominion Day, July 1, 1904.

THE CHARLES ZINCK HOUSE, BRISTOL AVENUE, C.1900

This unique house sits on Bristol Avenue, across the bridge from the main part of Liverpool. It was built by Charles W. Zinck, who was a commercial representative of a Halifax company, A. and W. Smith and Company. In 1900 Zinck married a Brooklyn girl, Lela Crooks, daughter of Captain William Crooks. When the Zincks celebrated their fifteenth wedding anniversary in 1915, the newspapers spoke of their beautiful home, and told how the archways and bay windows were festooned with apple blossoms and white lilacs, while the rooms were adorned with roses and carnations. Zinck died in 1941.

The house is owned today by writer and artist Marjorie Speed, best known for her children's book *Alexander's Sky Blue Eggs*. She and her late husband came to Liverpool in 1982. The photograph, donated by Gary Hartlen, is in the collection of the Queens County Museum.

THE CAPTAIN JOSEPH BARSS HOUSE, C.1930

The first Captain Barss was at the helm of the schooners *Enterprise* and *Despatch*, among the earliest of the legendary Liverpool privateers. When living in this house, Captain Barss' son Joseph Barss Jr. was born. Joseph Barss Jr. grew up to be one of the most famous of the privateer captains, commanding the *Liverpool Packet*, which made close to two hundred captures of enemy vessels in its days on the high seas.

Privateer vessels both protected the coast of Nova Scotia and harassed enemy vessels. They were funded by private citizens and manned by Liverpool men, many of whom went on to distinguished public lives once their privateering days were over. After his days of glory and his eventual capture and imprisonment in New England, Joseph Barss Jr. was allowed to return to Nova Scotia on the condition that he no longer be involved in privateering. He eventually took up farming in Kentville, but missed the ocean and his fellow privateers. He was unsuccessful as a farmer and died at the young age of 49, and is buried, wrote historian Janet Mullins, "in the shadow of oaks, in the beautiful Kentville cemetery, far from his sea-side home, and the resting place of any of his fellow-rovers."

The Captain Joseph Barss house is now Lane's Privateer Inn, opened by innkeeper and long-time Liverpool Mayor Ron Lane in October, 1962. The house had been bought by J.Edgar Lane, Ron's father, in 1947 and housed businesses such as a furniture store, beauty parlour, and coffee shop. General manager of the inn now is Lane's daughter, Susan.

THE JUD YOUNG HOUSE, MAIN STREET, LIVERPOOL C.1900S

This handsome property in Liverpool, located at 313 Main Street, was owned by Judson A. Young. He had been born in Mill Village and had worked there with the firm of I.N. Mack until moving to Liverpool, where he opened a boot and shoe business. He carried on that business until just two years before his death, in 1929. His obituary was elegantly written: "In business he was the soul of honour, and gave value in every sale he made. Upon this principle he gained the patronage of a large territory, and customers always returned to him to do their purchasing." The house still stands, though the verandah has been removed and the clapboard covered.

THE DR. JORDAN WESLEY SMITH HOUSE, C.1900S

THE DR. JORDAN WESLEY SMITH HOUSE UNDER CONSTRUCTION, C.1900S

46   HISTORIC QUEENS COUNTY

The Dr. Jordan Wesley Smith House, c.1900s

The imposing home shown at left is on one of Liverpool's busiest corners, and now serves as the location of shops and businesses. It was built by Dr. Jordan Wesley Smith, who was born in Hants County, Nova Scotia, in 1864 and who died in 1948, a year after he retired from medical practice. The photograph at bottom left by Gilbert Kempton shows the house under construction, and the photograph below shows Dr. Smith's office, probably put up just after the great fire of 1895. Dr. Jordan Smith had the house built in 1900.

Dr. Smith began his career as a teacher in Baddeck and Milton, went to medical school in Baltimore, practiced there for a short time, did post-graduate work in New York, then returned to Nova Scotia to practice briefly in Port LaTour. Then he took up a practice in Liverpool, which he ran continuously almost to his death. He married Alma Hunt of South Brookfield, and is buried there with her. The photograph of the house is taken from *Beautiful Queens*, published first in 1903 and reprinted in 1993 by the Queens County Museum, which also has the other two photographs in its collection.

DR. SMITH'S OFFICE—A WOODEN SHACK—PUT UP AFTER THE FIRE OF 1895.

LANDMARKS PAST AND PRESENT

CHESTNUT HALL, THE PATCH-WATSON RESIDENCE, LIVERPOOL, C.1920S

A large chestnut tree stood in front of this lovely old residence on the main street of Liverpool, giving it the name of Chestnut Hall. The home belonged to Thomas E.D. Watson and his wife Mary Laura "Mollie" (Patch). Thomas, who was originally from Scotland, was living in New York when he married Mollie, who was born and brought up in Liverpool. They moved to Liverpool after World War One. Thomas was born in 1879 and died in 1945; Mollie was born in 1875 and died in 1972. Thomas Watson was involved with the Children's Aid Society in Liverpool and with the Boy Scouts; he also wrote a number of articles on the Social Credit movement.

Chestnut Hall, in which the author Thomas Raddall once rented an apartment, is another example of a heritage property being carelessly discarded. In 1962 the house was torn down and a squat, utilitarian liquor commission put in its place. The local newspaper lamented the loss of the house, "one of the fine old properties on Main Street. The old marble fireplaces and some nice old timbers must be taken down but that is all in the name of progress."

FORT POINT, LIVERPOOL, 1905

This photograph shows Fort Point, the point of land that guards Liverpool Harbour, and its lighthouse, built in 1855 and first lit on New Year's night, 1856. Janet Mullins, writing in 1941, said that in no other part of Liverpool had groups of people experienced such varied and poignant emotions as on this small headland. "It has been the scene of love, hate, treachery, greed, loyalty, fear, grief, thievery and cruel floggings." Today it is a park, a tranquil place of lawns and a lighthouse, with a view across the bay of Brooklyn and the Bowater Mersey Paper Company.

As Mullins said, it was not always so. "Almost every day," she said, "privateers came into the harbour, some of the bolder into the river having rounded the Point. The frightened and angry spectators saw them chasing our vessels, throwing their cargoes overboard, or reloading it on their own vessels; firing upon them on Herring Cove, on Black Point, on the Point and the Town; saw them taking away men from the shore, from craft in the harbour and loot from houses, stores, wharves and shipping." Liverpool privateers in turn chased the enemy, devastating New England shipping, and as they left on their raids people would see them off from Fort Point.

THE TUNA INN AND WOBAMKEK BEACH SUMMER RESORT, C.1920S

The white sand beaches of the South Shore have always attracted travellers, and local people have accommodated them in a variety of ways. The postcard shown here was an advertisement for the Tuna Inn, Hunts Point (there was an earlier Tuna Inn on Great Island, off Port Medway). An advertisement in *The Advance* said that the Tuna Inn was ready for business, its cottages spic and span and the dining room and coffee bar ready for regular meals or snacks. By 1966, according to Tim McDonald, nothing remained to indicate that the Tuna Inn had ever been there. Its cabins had all been sold and moved to other locations, and private cabins had been built where the inn once had been.

Another interesting draw for tourists was the Wobamkek Beach Summer Resort, located in Port Mouton, begun in 1922, and called one of the loveliest spots for a summer resort in Canada. Advertisements said it was only ten minutes drive from the Canadian National Railway station, hotel, and store. The resort had a central dining room of log construction, said the brochures, and a golf course laid out over the sand fields, between the cottages and the sea. Built by J.W. Willis, it was located near the spot where Champlain was said to have set up his base for exploring the coast. Besides golf, guests could take part in moose and deer hunting, duck hunting, plus trout and tuna fishing.

Cabins for Wobamkek were made of frame construction, no plaster, and finished inside with planed boards. Each cabin had its own fireplace and contained as well a living room, kitchenette, and from two to four bedrooms. A season's rental would cost between $225 and $300.

THE 1785 PATRICK DORAN HOUSE, MILL VILLAGE, 1958

This is one of the oldest houses in Queens County. Notes with this E.G.L. Wetmore photograph in the Provincial Archives say that it took four years to build this house, back in the 1780s. "The basement walls, four feet thick, are of hand cut stones, the centre of the basement is filled with a solid mass of rock about ten feet square which serves as a base for the huge fireplace chimney which rises through the centre of the building. Some of the wall and floor planks are 24 inches wide, while the original pegs, hand wrought hinges and old brass locks can still be seen on all the doors. The hand carving and square wall panelling are particularly noteworthy features of the house; a skilled workman was brought especially from Connecticut, and spent two years working on the project. The present house boasts the four original fireplaces, plus the original well."

The house was originally built by Desire Mack after her husband, lumberman Samuel Mack, died in 1783. Patrick Doran, born in Waterford, Ireland, and who had been a chief clerk first to Simeon Perkins then to Samuel Mack, married Desire in 1785. As *South Shore; Seasoned Timbers* puts it, he became a lumberman with a good-sized home farm. A daughter of the Dorans married a Davison, a family name connected with the house for the next one hundred years. Grandson Edward Doran Davison was one of the important lumbermen of southwestern Nova Scotia. In 1920 the house was purchased by Gavin Creed, son of Frederick Creed, who was the inventor of the teleprinter and whose family founded Creeds, a famous Toronto store. In the 1950s the house changed ownership again and became the Medway Inn; today it is a private residence.

CAPTAIN AMOS SABEAN HOUSE, PORT MEDWAY, C.1915

Both Amos and his brother Thaddeus were captains living in Port Medway. This photograph shows Captain Amos Sabean's house in Port Medway. A list of qualified electors for District Number 8, dated 1886, shows Amos, Thaddeus, and their father, Isaiah all listed as electors. The house shown here was across the street from three stores: Morine's, Bowlby's, and Clement's. Captain Sabean was but one of many captains who called Port Medway home. As Marguerite Letson wrote, back in the 1860s Port Medway was a busy seaport. "Ships from all the ports along the coast, more especially from Liverpool and Yarmouth, loaded ton timber, lumber and deals for the West Indies, South Africa and Great Britain, while a flourishing trade was carried on with Boston and other parts of the U.S.A."

Letson went on to reminisce about the captains in the community when she was young, describing each. Some lived long lives—-she says of Captain George Chisholm that he lived to a good old age and lies in the little graveyard, overlooking the blue waters that were so long his home—but many died at sea. When Captain Edward Cohoon's barque *E. W. Cohoon* was run down by a topsail schooner, Captain Cohoon and all but one of the crew went down with the ship. Marguerite Letson writes that "Back your rope-sails, we're sinking" were the last words of, as she put it, as gallant a seaman as ever sailed blue water.

THE ISAIAH LESLIE RESIDENCE, PORT MOUTON, C.1911

The beautiful home shown in this Gilbert Kempton photograph still exists, not much changed in almost a hundred years. Isaiah was said to be a descendant of Jasper Leslie, who was one of the original 20,000 Loyalists to arrive in Nova Scotia after the American Revolution. The Loyalists who settled Port Mouton were disbanded soldiers who had been members of a British Legion commanded by Bonastre Tarleton. As M. Marie Woodworth describes in *The Early History of Port Mouton*, at the end of the war the Loyalists gathered their families and belongings and came to Nova Scotia, where they chose to lay out a township in what is now Port Mouton. They named the township Guysborough, after Sir Guy Carleton. It consisted of close to 19,000 acres of land and was said to have contained three hundred houses and more than eight hundred people. The Loyalists chose their land by drawing a chit from a hat. Some of these original chits can be seen in the Queens County Museum. Many settlers found the soil around Port Mouton difficult for farming. Woodworth reports that in February 1784 a number of the settlers were discontented with their land around Port Mouton and looked elsewhere for land that would be suitable for settlement. Some left to settle both Guysborough County and the area which became St. Stephen, New Brunswick.

Isaiah Leslie was born in Port Mouton, spent some time as manager of a lobster factory in Lockeport and later spent many years in the mercantile life of Port Mouton. He married Edith Dexter of Milton and died at the age of sixty-three. A column in the local newspaper, *The Advance*, described how he died, trying to retrieve a bucket that had fallen into a well. "On Thursday morning early he made the attempt, the curb being removed, but it would seem one of the stones of the well gave way, and Mr. Leslie, who had been subject to faint spells, was no doubt unable to recover his balance, and must have fallen in head-foremost."

THE SCOTIA HOUSE, PORT MOUTON, C.1910S

One of the fondly-remembered coastal accommodations for tourists and travellers in the early 1900s was the Scotia House, which occupies a place at the centre of Port Mouton's history. An early advertisement said the Scotia House would be opened on Thursday, June 20, 1907. "The Scotia House," the advertisement read, "has just been built, is well-furnished with bath and other conveniences. Only two minutes walk from the H & S-W station. Teams provided at any time."

Thaddus Mehlman, who died not long ago at the age of ninety-nine, was interviewed by the local newspaper when he was ninety-three. He said that if you could have seen Port Mouton eighty years ago, you wouldn't think it was the same place. In the late 1890s and early 1900s, he said, Port Mouton was a thriving community, supporting a number of industries and businesses. There was a sawmill on Broad River, at least three lobster processing factories, and one fish plant. "And right in the middle of the community, in the midst of all the activity, was the old Scotia House." The Scotia House shown in this photograph, courtesy of Carol Doggett, burned down in the 1920s. A second Scotia House was built in 1923 but was eventually demolished.

WHITE POINT BEACH LODGE, C.1930S

PHOTOS AT RIGHT

One of the most important Nova Scotian coastal resorts today is White Point Beach Resort, located at the top of the eastern side of Port Mouton Bay. These photographs of the exterior of the lodge and its dining room show it in its early years. It was built between 1928 and 1929 by Phil H. Moore, who had a place on Lake Rossignol before the area was taken over by the Mersey Power development. A story in the *Halifax Daily Star* in May of 1929 said that construction of the lodge and a series of log cabins nearby was proceeding rapidly. "The main lodge will have all modern summer hotel equipment," the story said, "and even the log cabins will be equipped with bath, electric lights and telephone with a cheery open fireplace for September nights. It promises to be one of the most attractive summer places on the whole South Shore."

Today White Point Beach Resort is a major provincial convention centre and boasts an excellent beach, golf course, swimming pools, and hiking trails. The old log cabins, updated, stand side by side with other resort cabins and new accommodation pavilions, which have views of the ocean and the lake.

THE N.F. DOUGLAS HOUSE, CALEDONIA, 1890s

Nelson Foster Douglas was an important merchant and landowner in North Queens at the turn of the last century and his business, N.F. Douglas and Company Limited, continues today as one the primary economic engines of the area. These photographs show Douglas' house on the West Caledonia Road, which he built in 1887. Nelson is the man seated on the left, with the child on his knee. Nelson was the son of Milton Douglas, who started a small store in 1875 to serve the families of the men who worked in the woods for him, and the grandson of John Douglas, one of the first settlers in the Northern District. Nelson married Lennie Freeman of Harmony. Two of their five children were Lee and Perry, who ran the business together after their father's death in 1914. Lee married a beautiful Lunenburger named Mabel Millet and built a house next to the N.F. Douglas house. Lee and Mabel were the parents of now-retired Halifax doctor Betty Ross and of the second Nelson F. Douglas, who married Muriel Swindell of Berwick. Nelson owned and operated the N.F. Douglas and Company business until his death in 1992. The N.F. Douglas house is now gone, but today's owner of the business, Nelson and Muriel Douglas's son Blair, lives with his wife Jean and family in the Lee and Mabel Douglas house next door.

CALEDONIA'S ALTON HOUSE, 1902

Located just off the Caledonia corner and standing today is Caledonia's Alton House, once a well-known hotel catering to those making the journey from Liverpool to Annapolis, and to those coming into the area for gold mining, hunting, and fishing. Stagecoaches left the hotel daily for Liverpool and Annapolis. Leone Smith's history of Caledonia says that it was built by Jonas Parker in 1860 and was run by a succession of people, including "a Captain Ennis" of Liverpool. By 1896 it was owned by James McGuire, who hired the carpenter Arthur Boucher—the man who built Liverpool's Town Hall—to modify the building. The next owner was Nathaniel Harlow, who traded his farm in Harmony for the hotel and sold it to Byron Kempton in 1902. This picture was taken around that time. The hotel remained in the Kempton family for the next several decades and was operated as a hotel for many years. Even today it periodically changes hands with people making plans to restore it to its former glory. The original sign for the Alton House is still in existence, and the back is signed by Gilbert Kempton, who, besides taking some of the early photographs of Liverpool, was a noted sign painter.

Kedgemakooge Lodge, c.1915 and a cabin at the lodge, c.1940s

The heavily-used areas of Kejimkujik National Park lie partly in Queens County and partly in Annapolis County, and while the old Kedge Lodge was a few hundred metres inside Annapolis County, the economic focus of the area has always been as much towards Caledonia as it has been to any other community in Nova Scotia. Many of the people who worked in the area of what is now the national park lived in Queens County, and their children—at least after consolidation— went to schools in Caledonia. Travelogues about Nova Scotia in the 1920s called Caledonia the gateway to the famous Rossignol and Kedgemakooge countries. It would be wrong to have a history of Queens County that did not mention this area, so vital to its life.

These photographs show the original Kedge Lodge and one of the cabins, some of which were privately owned by members of the lodge. People from New England and the rest of the Maritimes came each year for hunting, fishing, and the natural beauty.

The Fairy Lake area of northern Queens and south Annapolis counties was a special area of the Mi'kmaq for thousands of years. In recognition of this fact, Kejimkujik National Park now adds "and National Historic Site" to its name, the historic designation being given to recognize the area's Mi'kmaq history. By 1900, however, there were no Mi'kmaq living around Fairy Lake. In 1908 an Annapolis Royal man, Clarence Will Mills, obtained a lease for

land from the Department of Indian Affairs. By 1909 Kedge Lodge, originally called the Kedgemakooge Rod and Gun Club, was open. That particular lodge was destroyed by fire seven years later and quickly rebuilt, though the new lodge was not quite as grand as its predecessor. The lodge passed to different owners, the final ones being Norm and Thelma Bowers, who ran the lodge until it was expropriated for the national park in the 1960s.

Hotels in Greenfield for fishermen and hunters, c.1930s and 1940s

The number of cars parked around the Freeman House in the 1940s shows how popular the area was as a destination from the turn of the century for hunters and fishermen from both New England and around the province. A manuscript history of Greenfield, written by Janet Wile, says that a house built by Ladd Burnaby had been used as a boarding house and changed hands a number of times. Around 1900 it was sold to Boardman Hunt, "and it became known as the Maple Leaf Hotel," shown at left in this photo from the the Dewey Photographic Studio, Chatham, New Brunswick and contained in the DesBrisay Museum collection in Bridgewater. "When Link Hunt came home from World War One," Wile wrote, "he remodelled it in 1920 into a three storey building. It would seem the tourist industry had begun in earnest." This hotel was bustling with fishermen in the spring. Tragically, at four o'clock on February 22, 1938, the people of Greenfield were aroused by the sound of horns honking and the yell of "fire." The Maple Leaf was burning. "A bucket brigade was quickly formed," a report said, "but despite all efforts made the hotel lies a complete mass of ashes."

The Freeman House was opened by Earl Freeman in 1926. Freeman had been a guide at the Maple Leaf before branching off on his own. Wile says additions were added and there was a suite set aside for rich Americans who came to Greenfield each year. Since there was no electricity at the time, power was provided by batteries charged by gasoline motors. In the photo below, the Freeman House is shown during the 1940s.

59 LANDMARKS PAST AND PRESENT

The legendary Pinehurst—beauty and mystery, c.1908

Not far from Cameron's Landing, at the south end of South Brookfield and on a hill overlooking the Christopher Lakes, stands what is left of Pinehurst, a lodge built by A. Byron McLeod, great-great grandson of the Camerons, who gave their name to the area. Sitting among tall trees on 100 acres of land, Pinehurst was the site of countless visits, dinners, and gatherings over the years, as McLeod entertained friends from far and wide. There were tennis courts, volleyball courts, fishing, hunting, hiking, and water activities. There was even a book published in Boston in 1908 called *Pinehurst or Glimpses of Nova Scotia Fairyland*, written by R.R. McLeod and containing photographs by A. Byron McLeod (his nephew). The photographs on these pages show Byron McLeod sitting by the fire at Pinehurst, and an outside view of the back of the lodge.

Pinehurst from the back, showing the tennis courts

In 1924 Byron McLeod sold Pinehurst to Lou Keytes, a businessman from the United States. Keytes quickly became a popular figure in both north and south Queens. He hired people to renovate Pinehurst and entertained and spent lavishly. He made friends with George Banks, the editor of *The Gold Hunter*, who often drove him about. He joined the Royal Nova Scotia Yacht Squadron in Halifax and moved among the city's elite. According to *Brookfield in the Wilderness*, his parties at Pinehurst were spectacular, with Keytes once entertaining his guests with the Boston Symphony Orchestra.

A. Byron McLeod in front of the fire at Pinehurst

Author Thomas H. Raddall was one of those who knew Keytes, describing him as fortyish, bald, with a bushy black beard. He had been to Pinehurst to visit Keytes. "I was one of the young people who enjoyed his parties there, travelling with fortunate friends who had cars." Then, one day Keytes took his coat to a Halifax tailor, who noticed the name Leo Koretz sewn inside. The name rang a bell with the tailor, something to do with a land and investment swindle. He alerted the appropriate provincial authorities, who in turn alerted Chicago authorities. A few days later, Leo Koretz, alias Lou Keytes, was arrested and taken back to the United States for trial. Before he served his sentence, however, Koretz, a diabetic, committed suicide by eating a box of chocolates.

Chapter 3

The Sea and the Land

FISHING, SHIPBUILDING, FARMING, FORESTRY, MINING, AND INDUSTRY

LIVERPOOL WATERFRONT, C.1910

A note in the Queens County Museum says that in the early 1900s Liverpool Harbour generally had around eighty vessels at anchor, each vessel with between fourteen and seventeen men. In this photograph, taken by Gilbert Kempton, the ship seen in the foreground is the S.S. *McElwain*, which belonged to the Sable River Lumber Company. A Norwegian steamer is loading pulp and a tern schooner, the *H.R. Silver*, is loading timber for foreign ports.

SHIPS DOCKED AT THE LIVERPOOL WATERFRONT, 1907

Liverpool was once one of the most important towns in Nova Scotia. For a number of years after settlement in the latter part of the 1700s, it was perhaps the second most important community after Halifax. At a time when a community's wealth could be extracted from the sea and the land, Liverpool prospered. Mayor and later Sheriff D.C. Mulhall, born in 1866, said he could remember Liverpool as a great shipping port rated as the fourth largest in Canada, with about 350 vessels of all tonnages registered there. "The docks extended a mile from Shipyard Point to Fort Point," he said, in *Some Liverpool Chronicles*. "Upwards of seven shipyards were in operation, employing hundreds of skilled ship carpenters." This Gilbert Kempton photograph shows some of that activity.

Thomas H. Raddall spoke of this time—and of the reasons for Liverpool's decline from this status—in his autobiography. "During the prime of 'wooden ships and iron men,' Liverpool was busy launching windjammers and sending them in the carrying trade around the world" he wrote in *In my Time: A Memoir*.

"A few miles above Liverpool at the head of tidewater, Milton's sawmills prospered on the export trade to the West Indies and South America." Raddall said that the United States financial panic of 1873-74 ruined both banks and business in Queens County. "At this point in time the wooden windjammer was doomed by iron and steam. During the previous half century the lumbermen had cut most of the tall white pine that once covered a large part of the Mersey watershed." Raddall said there was plenty of other wood in the forest but that white pine was what the overseas market wanted. "By 1876 nearly all of the old established shipping and lumbering firms in the county were bankrupt, and their employees were penniless." Not all business activity ceased, of course. Shipbuilding went on, mills kept operating. It was not until the 1920s, however, when the Mersey Pulp and Paper Company built its huge pulp and paper mill, that good times returned.

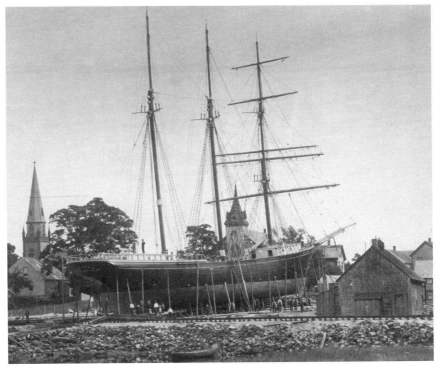

THE J.C. INNES SHIPYARD, 1903

This 1903 photograph shows the three-masted sailing ship *Milton* in the J.C. Innes Shipyard, in Liverpool. The J.C. Innes Shipyard was in operation just beyond the boom years of shipbuilding in Liverpool. In the years between the mid-1800s and 1920s shipyards in Liverpool built over 75,000 tons of shipping vessels. Seventeen shipyards were in operation in that time in Liverpool harbour and in the surrounding communities of Queens County. One of Liverpool's most famous mayors, D.C. Mulhall, himself involved in shipping, once said that there was such a congestion of shipping in Liverpool "that a pedestrian could walk from Liverpool to Bristol [the name given to the part of Liverpool lying north of the bridge across the harbour] by stepping from deck to deck of the vessels that filled the river."

63   THE SEA AND THE LAND

**SHIP-
BUILDING
IN
LIVERPOOL,
C.1890**

The ocean and ships were important to the communities along the South Shore. Almost from the moment of its inception, Liverpool men were building ships and sending them out on the ocean. In 1789 the principal ship owners of the port were Benjamin Collins, Simeon Perkins, Joseph Barss, Snow Parker, Elisha Hopkins, Ebenezer Harrington, Ebenezer MacLeod, William Gardner, and Ebenezer Dexter. It was said, in the 1880s, that Liverpool was one of the foremost harbours in Maritime Canada. Hector MacLeod, who was the son of master shipbuilder Robie MacLeod, wrote a paper on shipbuilding where he listed the master shipbuilders of the county as Ichabod Darrow (who built the *Rover*), George Gardner, Mathias MacLeod, Alexander McLaughlin, Jason Leslie, John MacLeod, Eliza Dolliver, Jason Gardner, Edward Gardner, Matthew MacLeod, Joseph Dexter, A. Boucher, J. Stedman Gardner, and Robie MacLeod. This photograph, in the Public Archives of Nova Scotia, was taken in 1890 by a photographer from Yarmouth and was found among family pictures in Liverpool by Mrs. Edith Mulhall Achilles.

THE J.N. RAFUSE AND SONS SHIPYARD, LIVERPOOL, C.1912

SMALLER PHOTOS,
AT RIGHT

One of the many firms involved in building ships in Queens County in the early years of the last century was J.N. Rafuse and Sons, Liverpool. The Rafuse shipyards were located on the Bristol Avenue approach to the bridge over the harbour. These two photographs, from the DesBrisay Museum, show a large, unidentified ship nearing completion, and the blacksmith shop and planing mill. The book *Sawpower*, by Barbara Robertson, notes that the Rafuse company had both a band saw and planer by 1912, used for cutting, bevelling, and smoothing timbers and planks for ship construction. It said that the equipment was normally installed outdoors, protected by a roof, to allow room to handle long, heavy timbers.

SHIPYARD POINT, LIVERPOOL, 1911

This photograph, taken by Gilbert Kempton, shows the three-masted schooner *David C. Ritcey* being built at Shipyard Point, in Liverpool. The *David Ritcey* apparently stuck on the ways when being launched, considered a sign of bad luck. She was built by master shipbuilder Robie MacLeod and launched in 1911, a tern schooner displacing about three hundred tons. Many ships were built on this spot, now the somewhat inglorious site of the Liverpool primary sewage treatment plant. At one time used by Simeon Perkins for ship building, the Point lost its value to shipping when the current bridge across the harbour was built without a section which could move to allow vessels to enter the inner harbour. Shipyard Point was owned by Robie MacLeod and was still in operation as late as 1920. It was even used during the World War Two to build scows for the federal government.

J.N. RAFUSE AND SONS SHIPYARD, LIVERPOOL, C.1912

THE SEA AND THE LAND

CROWDS WATCH THE *J.C. Hamlen* **BEING LAUNCHED, 1890**

Captain Lewis Sponagle's shipyard built the 535-ton brigantine *J.C. Hamlen* in the Bristol yard near Captain Joseph Barss's home. On the day she was launched in December of 1890, crowds lined the bridge across the Mersey to watch her come down the skids and into the harbour. Many thought she was the finest vessel ever launched in Liverpool, though later on she was said to look better than she handled. The shipyard had put down the keel of the *Hamlen* in April and between then and the launching, twenty-five men had been working daily on her construction. She was 125 feet long and 32 feet wide. Designed by Sponagle, her construction was supervised by master shipbuilder James Leslie. Much of the ship was built with native pine, while the cabins were finished in native hardwoods. A description of the launching in the files of the Queens County Museum said that extra precautions had to be taken in launching a ship of this size, with special buffers of large evergreen trees, including the branches, lining the wharves on the opposite shore. "As soon as she had left the ways, an anchor was dropped. When the ship brought up on the buffer, she was hauled back to pick up her anchor, and then docked at Ryan's wharf, just above the scene of her launching."

FISHING BOAT BUILT FOR JERRY V. NICKERSON BY LIVERPOOL WOODWORKING COMPANY, 1917

The famous Cape Island fishing boats of southwestern Nova Scotia owed much to Jerry V. Nickerson, who was one of a small group of Clark's Harbour fishermen working to produce a fishing and lobstering boat that could be used in the rough waters off the coast. Nickerson, born in Clark's Harbour in 1887, went to work at the age of twelve to support his fatherless family. In 1914 he and his two brothers Rosswell and Hubert established a fish-buying business on Cape Island and in 1916 moved it to Coffin's Island, in the mouth of Liverpool Harbour. A year later Jerry had this boat built for him by the Liverpool Woodworking Company. In 1920 Nickerson moved his business to Liverpool itself, setting up shop near the bridge across the Mersey River. Because he had a reputation for dealing fairly with fishermen, he was able to prevail in the competition to acquire the catches from the local boats. In 1928 he took over the North American Storage Company and then bought the Seven Seas Fishery Company. By 1932, Jerry, Rosswell, and Hubert formed a family company under the name of Nickerson Brothers. The company operated under that name until it was destroyed by fire in 1956, at which time Jerry retired from business. At one time a Liverpool town councillor, he had "a long and consistent record of honest and successful affairs, rarely equalled on this coast," said the newspapers. The photograph is from the collection of the Queens County Museum.

E.D. DAVISON AND SONS SAWMILLS ON THE MEDWAY, MILL VILLAGE, 1890

Edward Doran Davison was born in 1819 in Mill Village and by the time he died in 1894 the lumber company he founded was the largest producer of lumber in Nova Scotia. This photograph shows one of the mills Davison owned at Mill Village with his son Frank (standing at left). By 1890, when this photograph was taken, his company operated five waterpowered gang mills. Besides the two at Mill Village, there were two mills on the LaHave River at Bridgewater and a mill in Annapolis County on the Nictaux River. In her history of sawmills, Barbara Robertson notes that the mill in Annapolis County had twenty-eight upright saws, eight circular saws, and sixty saws in reserve. The Davison mills produced sixteen million board feet of lumber the year before Davison died.

Davison was not just involved in water-powered sawmills. He claimed to have owned the first steam-powered sawmill in the province—a claim open to interpretation. Robertson says that though Davison may or may not have operated the first steam sawmill, "he most certainly operated a sawmill by the first steam engine built in Nova Scotia outside the mines." Because of the steam produced by the mill it was always called the Old Kettle Mill; today one can still travel on the Old Kettle Road. Davison had the engine built in Dartmouth in 1845 and ended up using it at his gold mine in Molega, but not until after it had powered the Old Kettle Mill for many years. Robertson quotes him as saying that he had built the steam mill out of the foolishness of youth and patriotic ambition. Representing Queens County, Davison was elected a Liberal member of the provincial government in 1854. In 1865 he moved to Bridgewater, apparently as a result of the destructive forest fires that ravaged most of Queens County that year.

MILLS AT THE BRIDGE AT MILTON, C.1900

When you stand on the spot from where this photograph was taken over one hundred years ago, you see none of the mills that appear in this picture. They have all disappeared, replaced by a scenic landscape containing a park, a picturesque falls, and a blacksmith shop museum. Across the bridge on the right, a new restaurant with a terrace overlooking the river, was constructed in 2001 on the site of the Alister Harlow photo studio, the white building in the photograph. The railway no longer runs here and ships can no longer get upriver to load lumber. In the 1870s, Queens County had forty-two different sawmills, thirteen of which produced a million or more board feet of lumber a year. Milton had a good number of these, running on both water power and later steam. The mill on the left in this photograph belonged to Freeman Tupper, then Henry Tupper. It was built on the site of the first sawmill in Queens County, erected in 1760 just after Liverpool was founded.

THE COFFIN ISLAND LIGHT HOUSE, C.1900

Named after Peleg Coffin, one of the earliest settlers, Coffin Island guards the entrance to Liverpool Harbour. It was the site of activity in the fishing industry from the time that Nicholas Denys attempted to establish a fishery there in the 1630s and was of major importance to fishermen from the moment Liverpool was founded. Fish were dried on the island and rocks from its beaches were used as ballast for fishing schooners heading for the Grand Banks and the West Indies. The lighthouse in this picture was built in 1815, after the local Justices of the Peace, including Simeon Perkins, decided to commission the lighthouse in 1811. Perkins, at the age of seventy-six, helped to lay the cornerstone. Construction continued through the war of 1812, with the light being lit for the first time in 1816. The Coffin Island Lighthouse Heritage Society notes that the lighthouse was the fifth lighthouse built in Nova Scotia and the first to contain a revolving light, which was powered by whale oil. When the light was first built it stood ninety feet from the sea wall, but by 1876 the relentless effects of the sea had already put it in danger, necessitating the building of cribwork. On June 19, 1913, lightning struck the light and burned both it and the lighthouse keeper's house to the ground. A new lighthouse was built in 1914, this time 150 feet from the shore. It was closed in 1961 and today is the focus of preservation efforts, as the sea continues to eat away the shore. The Coffin Island Heritage Society is dedicated to preserving the light.

THE MERSEY PAPER COMPANY MILL C.1940S

The 1800s were a time of great prosperity for the people of Queens County, with shipbuilding, forestry, and gold mining leading an economic boom. Hard times came with a financial collapse in the United States in the 1870s, which wiped out many Liverpool investors, the advent of steamships which strangled the wooden shipbuilding industry, and the end of the gold mining industry. Good times did not return again until the Mersey Paper Company set up shop in Brooklyn in 1929. Experiments in the mid-1800s in Nova Scotia to produce paper from pulp made from spruce showed promise, and by the turn of the century there were mills producing pulp on the Mersey, including the Acadia Pulp and Paper Company, on the Medway, at Charleston, and on McGowan Lake in Harmony Mills, operated by James Cushing. The pulp was shipped elsewhere to be turned into paper. Author Thomas H. Raddall, who worked in the Mersey mill offices at one time, wrote that the Acadia mill was acquired by a promoter named F.J.D. Barnjum, whose big dream was to build a large newsprint mill at the mouth of the Mersey, something which eventually caught the interest of financier Izaak Walton Killam. He saw the potential of water power close by vast stands of timber. Killam arranged the financing, hired Colonel C.H.L. Jones to run the plant, and built the Mersey Paper Company mill, with a payroll of 475 in its first year. As Raddall writes in his history of the mill, 500 people came to the opening of the mill on December 14, 1929, many of them on a special VIP train from Halifax. Killam died in 1955 and the next year the executors of his estate sold the mill to the Bowater Corporation, headquartered in England, for over fifty million dollars. Bowater had long been interested in the Mersey mill and already had mills in Newfound-land and in the United States. Bowater nurtured the mill into the enterprise it is today, eventually acquiring over 1,000 square miles of woodland, enough to supply wood to the mill in perpetuity.

MILL AT THE FALLS ON THE MERSEY RIVER, MILTON, C.1890

This photograph shows one of the mills on the Mersey River at Milton in the latter part of the nineteenth century. Known as the John Millard Mill, it was built in the centre of the river, with other mills flanking the shores. The Milton mills turned out sophisticated products. Besides producing all types of lumber for both house and shipbuilding, they were involved in the manufacture of doors, flooring, window sashes, furniture, butter churns, mouldings, material for barrels, plus boxes for candles, fish, lobsters, and candy.

EUREKA GRIST MILL, LIVERPOOL, C.1900

BOTTOM RIGHT

The grist mill in this Gilbert Kempton photograph was powered by a water turbine and sat on the Old Mill Brook. It was owned by E.D. More, a town councillor, who lived in the house to the left of the mill. In 1901 More was advertising that Eureka Mills was now "prepared to sell to the public corn meal manufactured from the best quality of American Corn and equal if not superior to any meal imported into Liverpool." Notes in the Queens County Museum also indicate that the mill may have processed wheat from Russia. More advertised that his prices at wholesale and retail were as low as could be offered anywhere else in Queens County, and that "you get full weight buying from us." In a wistful plea that echoes through the decades, he exhorted the public to encourage home manufacture by purchasing meal at the Eureka Mills, and offered custom grinding of oats, barley, and buckwheat.

THE *Luna* LOADS LUMBER IN PORT MEDWAY, 1907

TOP RIGHT

The logs from the Medway River hinterland were turned into lumber in mills along the Medway and taken to Port Medway, where they were shipped to ports around the world. This photograph at top right, in the possession of retired Trent University historian Alan Wilson, whose mother grew up in Mill Village, shows the sailing ship *Luna* loaded with lumber in the harbour at Port Medway in 1907. While once a booming seaport, active with fishing, shipping, and shipbuilding, economic activity had slowed by the time this picture was taken. *The Advance* had editorialized in 1897 that it was glad to see some attention being paid to Port Medway and that it was strange that the advantages of the port appear never to have struck anyone in the press. The newspaper hoped that once steamers got into the habit of visiting the port prosperity would revisit Port Medway, "that its streets will be filled with vehicles, its wharves busy with traffic, and its stores be full of wares and have lots of customers." The newspaper was even hoping that the coming railway would have a branch line connecting Port Medway with the village of Greenfield. The area spoken of here has a special appeal for Alan Wilson, who always connects it with his mother, Margaret (Madge) Graham. He says she had known the area "from her birth in Charleston to growing up there and in Mill Village, Port Medway and later, at Bridgewater." Her father, Walter Graham, had been manager for the Nova Scotia Pulp and Paper Company and later for the Edward Doran Davison lumber operations in Queens, Lunenburg, and Annapolis counties.

THE SEA AND THE LAND

THE SMITH MILLS AT HARMONY, C.1897

Different types of mills in Harmony made use of various water courses. The first mill over the Joe Tom Brook was a sawmill, built in 1819. The waterwheel mill in this photograph later occupied that site on the end of Harmony Lake, not far from the large pulp mill built by James Cushing on McGowan Lake. The grist mill portion was first built in the 1830s by Zoeth Freeman, but when it burned, Nathaniel Smith and James Cushing rebuilt it, also installing in 1872 the first rotary sawmill in the Northern District. The mill was eventually owned and operated by Nathaniel Smith alone.

Shirley Smith, Nathaniel's granddaughter, says the buildings in the mill complex on the left of the photograph, sitting over the dam, are the cider mill and the grist mill. Next to them is the sawmill, with its planer and lumber storage, the little building in front being the slipway; logs were sawn, planed, and stored in the rest of the building. For years it was run by Nathaniel's son, James Smith, who was born in 1893. His house, lived in today by his daughter Shirley Smith, can be seen next. The building on the right was the Freeman general store. While there was no carding mill among all of the mills, Nathaniel's brother Zenas Smith said in a diary that one had been built in Brookfield in 1832. Previous to that the wool had to be taken to Nictaux. Smith said the carding mill was a great boon, especially to women, who had always done the "very labourious work" of carding.

The grist mill at one time produced flour of a very high quality, being equipped with the best mill stones in the Northern District. Wagons pulled by oxen and piled high with wheat would line up for a mile to have the wheat threshed and ground. The grist mill burned in January, 1953, though the sawmill was saved—only to burn in 1962. James Smith rebuilt the mill and sold it the next year to Raymond and Paul Freeman of Caledonia. They kept it a few years, then sold it to Willis Forrest, who later owned the sawmill in Caledonia built by Bowater Mersey in 1963. Today, that mill is the N.F. Douglas Lumber Company mill, and the Harmony mill has passed into history. The photograph was donated by Shirley Smith and is in the collection of the North Queens Heritage House.

HARRY FREEMAN'S MILL IN GREENFIELD, BEFORE AND AFTER THE FLOOD, 1956

There have been mills in Greenfield as long as there has been settlement and the Freeman family has been associated with those mills from the beginning. Two years after the community was settled in 1830, Gorham Freeman built the first sawmill. Others followed. The success of the mills later attracted E.D. Davison, who got his start in Mill Village and went on to be the biggest lumber producer in the province. Davison planned to expand a mill he bought in Greenfield but his plans were contingent on the railway coming up from Liverpool. A trail was laid out but the railroad never came, and Davison moved on to other locations. The Freemans remained, however. In 1906 and 1907 Walter, Park, and Gus Freeman built a shingle mill, which ran from a water wheel. That mill operated until 1954, when Hurricane Edna destroyed it. Harry Cleveland Freeman, World War Two veteran, municipal councillor for twenty-five years, and father of the present founder and owner of the Harry Freeman and Sons company, rebuilt the mill, only to see it destroyed again by the great flood of January 1956. The photograph below shows all that was left of the mill after the flood. It was rebuilt yet again, this time in another spot and run by diesel engines. It was moved to its present location in 1965, burned in 1990, and was rebuilt. Harry Freeman died in 1982 at the age of eighty-nine, and his son, also called Harry C. Freeman, took over. Today the Harry Freeman and Sons mill is a modern mill ranking among the largest lumber producers in southwestern Nova Scotia.

THE SEA AND THE LAND

MEN IN A NORTHERN DISTRICT WOODS CAMP, C.1890S

Twelve men are shown at dinner time in a woods camp in the interior of southwestern Nova Scotia in this photograph, the original of which is in the North Queens Heritage House collection, donated from the McClare Collection, Hantsport. The woods boss is on the left and the camp cook on the right. Woods work was without question the most important industry in the interior from the time the district was settled to the present day. Men like these in the photograph would go into the woods camps in the fall and remain there all winter, returning home after the spring drives when the logs would be taken to the mills. Morrison and Friend, in their history, write that the food eaten in the camps was not fancy but it was filling. "Fresh meat from the surrounding forests, beans, bread, tea, and molasses were common." This fare, they said, was needed to fortify men working from dawn to dusk, six days a week. In *Woodchips and Beans,* Mike Parker interviews Greenfield logger Alan Hunt, who says the cook baked his bread with a reflector oven before an open fire, as in this photograph, then set up a bean hole to bake beans. Hunt said that on the river drives the loggers ate four meals a day, one before daylight, one in the middle of the morning, one in the afternoon, and the last after dark.

GOLD MINERS AND GOLD MINES AT MOLEGA DURING THE GREAT GOLD RUSH, 1888

PHOTOS AT RIGHT

After a substantial gold find was made at Whiteburn, in the Northern District, in 1884, prospectors searched the whole area hoping to strike it rich. Author, lawyer, and naturalist R.R. McLeod was also a geologist who at one point managed a mine in Mexico. In a history of the Northern District published in 1904, he writes that "the precious metal was found in a vein than ran through the ledges of an old pasture in North Brookfield," leading to the establishment of a major mining operation there. Soon after, prospectors came upon some rich "boulders" on a bit of wild land known as the "Molega Barrens."

By 1888 there were several mills at what came to be known as Molega Mines. The photo at bottom shows the Gilbert Parker and Nelson F. Douglas mine buildings under construction in 1888, and the photo below shows a man and woman in a rowboat on Ponhook Lake, with the Molega Mining Company mill and hotel in the background. Although the mine never did produce much of the gold mined in North Queens, it attracted a great deal of investment and saw the building of sophisticated mills. Close to twelve hundred people lived in Molega when the mines were in operation. By 1891 the mines were idle and the men laid off. Mining started up again in Molega a couple of years later and the area produced several thousand ounces of gold. A report in *The Advance* of July 7, 1897, noted that "C.U. McLeod, son of R.R. McLeod, deposited two bricks of gold with the Halifax Banking Company agency, Bridgewater, last week, taken from the Blue Mines, Molega, weighing 100 and 50 ozs. respectively." As the century ended production was declining and the mills closed.

GOLD MINERS AND GOLD MINES AT MOLEGA DURING THE GREAT GOLD RUSH, 1888

TRUCK OWNED BY JOHN SELDON, MOLEGA MINES, 1928

This photograph shows John Seldon's truck up on a ramp at the mining operation in Molega, which had a second breath of life in the late 1920s and on into the thirties. The building where the truck is parked is the shaft house and the one on the left is the boiler and stamp mill. While work had gone on intermittently at the mines, in 1938 a company owned by Colonel S.C. Oland began operations there and built a fifty-ton capacity ball mill. Production demanded large amounts of ore, however, so operations ended there in 1946.

In other areas the mines had been almost idle since the early 1900s, but there was a burst of activity in Whiteburn and Brookfield mines in the 1930s. Jim Morrison and Lawrence Friend, in their history of the western interior of Nova Scotia, speculate that this may have been due to the availability of labour during the depression. A ten-stamp mill was built by Lee and Perry Douglas in Whiteburn, eventually employing sixteen people, and lasting until 1941. In 1932 electric power from the Mersey development near Liverpool was run to the Brookfield Mines and the provincial government put up a mill with the daily capacity of twenty-five tons of ore. The mill was operational by 1934 but two years later it was short of capital and the mine was idle. In 1937 everything was destroyed by fire and mining ceased for good.

THE FREEMAN MILLS, LATER TIM STEWART'S CANOE FACTORY, SOUTH BROOKFIELD, C. 1888

PHOTOS AT RIGHT

Some of the finest wood and canvas canoes produced in Nova Scotia during the last century were made by Tim Stewart of South Brookfield. This photograph shows the Freeman mills on the Medway River, with the large building on the left eventually becoming Tim Stewart's shop. There are apparently few pictures of Tim Stewart at work, but the remains of the factory could be seen until just a few years ago. An advertising card for the business was located in the North Queens Heritage House.

Tim Stewart was born in 1877 and grew up in the area around Brookfield Mines, near North Brookfield. After working in the mines in Ontario he got a job at the Peterborough Canoe factory. Never one to be satisfied with the way something was done, he made a suggestion to the owners about a better way to design and build a canoe. They looked at it and said it could never be gotten off the mould. Tim Stewart left Ontario, came back to Nova Scotia, built the canoe and got it off the mould. In 1928 *The Gold Hunter* reported that he had produced twelve canoes since fall. For many years he turned out canoes from South Brookfield, said to be superior to any built in Peterborough. He built his last two canoes in 1945 and died in 1952.

THE FREEMAN MILLS, LATER TIM STEWART'S CANOE FACTORY, SOUTH BROOKFIELD, C.1888

THE JUMBO MINE AT WESTFIELD, C.1880S

If Brookfield was the first settlement in the interior of Queens County, Westfield came along soon after, as people from Brookfield moved upriver in search of sites for farms and mills. One of the first to move into the Northern District after William Burke was James Daley (sometimes called Dailey), who settled in the area. In 1888, gold was discovered in a seam in Westfield, promptly labelled the Jumbo Lead. In June of 1889 an English syndicate built a mine there, shown in this photograph, providing work for many in the local area. Shirreff's history of gold mining in Queens County says that the lode at Westfield was big, ranging in width from eight to twenty feet, but it failed to last for long. By 1903 the mine was being operated by Wilbur Libbey, of Boston, who had engaged the foreman of the New Germany Pulp Mill as manager, but it was closed a couple of years later.

THE NOVA SCOTIA WOODENWARE FACTORY, SOUTH BROOKFIELD, C.1930

In 1929, Prime Minister R.B. Bennett convinced his friend Charles Bienvenu to move his wooden box factory to Nova Scotia from Quebec, where it had become difficult to find the necessary raw materials. Bienvenu chose a spot on the banks of the Medway River in South Brookfield, and opened Nova Scotia Woodenware Limited in 1930. The factory was a huge boost to the economy of North Queens. Most of its more than one hundred workers were hired locally and several million board feet of lumber were used annually. The plant, dismantled in Quebec and rebuilt in South Brookfield, manufactured such items as wooden pails, candy pails, fish boxes, orange crates, egg crates, ammunition boxes, lard pails, pickle barrels, and many other kinds of containers.

In a magazine advertisement published in 1934, the company said it had found in Nova Scotia new opportunities, new economies, new resources, and new encouragement. It said that being contiguous to one of the finest stands of timber in the province, on a railway line, and near the sea gave it new advantages and economies in transportation. The company built several large, luxurious houses for its managers on the main road and smaller houses for its workers. The street on which the workers' houses were built came to be known, unsur-prisingly, as French Street, since workers who were not local came from Quebec. The company found South Brookfield such a friendly place that in its brochures it described the community as the "Place of Welcome," partly a play on Bienvenu's name.

On June 14, 1944, fire broke out in one of the mill buildings. The blaze was fought by fire departments from North Queens, Liverpool, and Bridgewater, but by the time the fire was brought under control most of the plant had been destroyed. Because it was difficult to replace the machinery in wartime, the plant closed.

PULP MILL AT CHARLESTON, BETWEEN MILL VILLAGE AND GREENFIELD, C.1910

This photograph shows the Nova Scotia Wood Pulp and Paper Company mill at Charleston, a small community a short distance up the Medway River from Mill Village. In its earliest days Charleston drew sustenance from lumber and gold. Several sawmills operated in the area, the limber being shipped to market through Port Medway. The gold was taken from narrow seams by the Gold Eagle Mining Company.

The Nova Scotia Wood Pulp and Paper Company mill was built in 1880. It was one of the first pulp mills in the province and was located on the site of earlier sawmills at Salter's Falls. Ralph Johnson's history of the forests of Nova Scotia notes that this mill burned in June of 1903 but that it was quickly rebuilt, the new mill being the one in the picture above. The pulp produced at the mill was taken by wagons and sleds pulled by horses and oxen to Port Medway, from where it made its way by steamers to the United States. When this mill was destroyed by fire in 1947, the business closed for good.

One of the problems facing the mill in its early days was a lack of water during the summer, meaning that the mill could only run about nine months of the year. In 1916 a dam was constructed by the mill owners, creating a pond to store water. When the mill burned for the final time, the site became a federal and provincial fish hatchery. This photograph is in the Tim McDonald collection.

Chapter 4

Transportation: Getting About

BOATS, TRAINS, WAGONS, AUTOMOBILES

EARLY TRANSPORTATION

Two earlier modes of transportation salute each other on the road from South Brookfield to Caledonia in the early 1900s. This photograph was found in the home of the late Mrs. Eva Cameron.

The City of St. John in Liverpool Harbour, c.1890s

Without railroad service and plagued by poor roads, people who wanted to travel found that one of the best ways to do so was by water. This paddle wheeler, the *City of St. John*, made the run up and down the coast from Yarmouth to Halifax. It would leave Yarmouth every Friday morning, stopping at Barrington, Shelburne, Lockeport, Liverpool, and Lunenburg. On its return voyage it left Pickford and Black's wharf in Halifax for intermediate points and would connect in Yarmouth with the steamer for Boston on Wednesday evenings.

It was a busy route, especially from Liverpool. The editor of *The Advance* made the case for serving Liverpool at a more reasonable hour, saying that the traffic to and from Liverpool exceeded the combined traffic from all of the other ports. "Under the circumstances," the newspaper said, in an editorial dated July 28, 1897, "we certainly think that Liverpool's convenience should be so far consulted as that the steamer should be timed to arrive here at reasonable hours, by day rather than by night."

FREIGHT AND PASSENGER PACKET SERVICE TO HALIFAX AND YARMOUTH, C.1900

This photograph by Gilbert Kempton shows a steamer packet leaving Bartling's wharf, Liverpool, on its run from Halifax to Yarmouth and return. D.C. Mulhall, later Liverpool mayor, then county high sheriff, served as agent for the service and advertised that the S.S. *Prince Edward* would leave at nine in the morning every Tuesday, arriving in Yarmouth Wednesday afternoon in time to make connections with the S.S. *Prince George* for Boston. For its return voyage the packet would wait in Yarmouth for the arrival of the S.S. *Prince Arthur* from Boston, then sail back. Rates were advertised as lower than on any other line, stateroom accommodations were said to be excellent, and the commissary was said to be unexcelled. Not only that, but the officials were advertised to be courteous and obliging.

LIVERPOOL AND MILTON TRAMWAY, 1898

This well-known photograph by N.D. Hammett was first published in a history of Queens County in a 1904 issue of *Acadiensis* courtesy of the Public Archives. It shows the little tram going along a wintry Main Street in Liverpool. A Massachusetts man, Frank Hutchinson, set up the tram to carry freight and passengers between Liverpool and Milton. He ordered the engine from England and had it shipped to Halifax, where it was put on a schooner for delivery in Liverpool. In a whimsical fashion the engine was covered with the shell of a Halifax trolley. The passenger car can be seen at the end of the train.

    The company was incorporated in 1896 with a number of Liverpool people listed as owners. It began operations on the first of February, 1897, hauling lumber, pulp, and passengers, the latter for a round trip fee of fifteen cents. The tracks ran down the centre of the road from the docks in Liverpool, along Main Street, then along the west side of the Mersey to Milton and its mills. In 1907 the line was bought by the Halifax and South Western Railway Company and rebuilt to match the gauge of the railway coming into Liverpool. When the Mersey Paper Company mill diminished the business of the pulp mills in 1929 in Milton, the line closed.

THE HALIFAX AND SOUTH WESTERN RAILWAY COMES TO LIVERPOOL, 1905

October 18, 1904 was called by diarist John Morton the most eventful day in the annals of Queens County. William S. Fielding, Member of Parliament for Queens and Shelburne and federal Minister of Finance, arrived in Liverpool by rail, a line which Morton said was "practically [Fielding's] own creation." Because the tracks hadn't as yet made it to Liverpool, Fielding got off in Brooklyn, following which there was a parade to town with a brass band and a procession of carriages. When Fielding's majority was reduced by twenty-six in the federal election the next month, Morton wrote that "so ungrateful is a thankless community that the man who has brought the Rail Road to our county has been politically stoned by hundreds of its inhabitants."

The photograph above shows the first passenger train in Liverpool, with the tracks not yet having crossed the road on their way to Yarmouth. Morton took a ride on the railway to Halifax in March of 1906. He used to make the trip from Liverpool to Bridgewater by buggy in five and a half hours, but the whole trip from Halifax to Liverpool, which left at 3:45 and arrived at 9:15 P.M, took the same amount of time. "I could scarcely believe it was possible as we glided along lounging on velvet cushions, where only a short time ago we were as long in getting from Bridgewater to Liverpool in the old coach over rough and muddy roads as we were making the whole journey."

TRANSPORTATION: GETTING ABOUT

KEEPING DOWN THE DUST, LIVERPOOL, C.1910S

A town water wagon loads water from a fire hydrant while a pair of young boys look on in this photograph taken by Gilbert Kempton. Information on the back of this picture says that the man shown may be John Dexter from Brooklyn, whose job it was to keep down the dust on the streets. An article in the Mersey Quarterly called *Liverpool in the Twenties* says that the streets of Liverpool during the 1920s were still unpaved, though they did have cement sidewalks where earlier there had been boardwalks. "In order to keep the dust down in summer, Isaac Whynot used to water the streets with a horse-drawn water-cart. Henry Hensey recalls that children would follow the cart and cool off under a shower from the sprinkler hoses." Henry Hensey was a beloved Liverpool character who today has a street named in his honour.

BUILDING THE TRAM LINE TO MILTON, 1899

PHOTOS AT RIGHT

These two photographs, taken in the same spot, show the Liverpool and Milton tram line being built up the west side of the Mersey River and the tram travelling along the line. Building the bed for the line was a slow process involving both manpower and horsepower, as the men lifting the rocks off the seven teams of horses would attest. In the background is Shipyard Point. Photographer Gilbert Kempton describes this as the beginning of the Nova Scotia Southern Railroad, November 1899.

The Halifax and South Western Railway bought the L and M Tramway in 1907, and once that happened the passenger service—where people could board in Milton and change trains in Liverpool for Yarmouth or Halifax—ended, and the rail line concentrated on carrying pulp for making paper.

BUILDING THE TRAM LINE TO MILTON, 1899

TAKEN FROM THE SAME SPOT, AFTER THE LINE WAS CORRECTED

TRANSPORTATION: GETTING ABOUT

A TEMPORARY BRIDGE OVER THE MERSEY, 1906

This Gilbert Kempton photograph, courtesy of the DesBrisay Museum in Bridgewater, shows one of the early trains on the Halifax and South Western Railway crossing a temporary bridge over the Mersey River. Duane Porter, one of the founders of a railway museum in Bridgewater devoted to the Halifax and South Western, said the line was known as the "Hellishly Slow and Wobbly." Information from the museum said that when the H&SWR was first built, many temporary wooden trestles such as this one were used but were replaced as soon as possible, in this case by 1908.

The diarist John Morton, a Milton lumberman, had been part of the committee sorting out the route for the railway. In July of 1902 he worried that the route chosen would be three or four miles upriver from Liverpool, heading on to Shelburne County and using the tramway as a connector. Morton said that would not do and that if the government failed to complete the railway at this time it would stand a poor chance of winning the next election. The issue became so contentious that Morton wrote that the best thing would be to extend the line from Bridgewater to Caledonia, already in operation, down to Milton and forget the route from Bridgewater to Liverpool for the time being. As far back as 1893, a company had been incorporated as the Atlantic and Inland Railway which would build a line from Liverpool through Indian Gardens, Brookfield, Caledonia, and on to Annapolis Royal, but nothing had come of it. Later the fear was that the Halifax and South Western Railway would miss Milton and its mills altogether, but Morton was confident that would not happen. Then, on May 11, 1905, he received a telegram from an engineer in Bridgewater that the railroad was to cross the river at Liverpool "and give Milton the smoke only. The news almost paralysed me." He said it was the greatest blow Milton had ever received and would mean the closing of the pulp mills.

WAITING FOR THE TRAIN, LIVERPOOL, C.1927

This photograph, from the National Archives in Ottawa, shows an ox and wagon waiting for the train in Liverpool. Linda Rafuse, curator of the Queens County Museum, collected information about the Liverpool train station from Clarence Nicol, who was the last train master of this station. Mr. Nicol said that when the station was first constructed, it was quite near the highway (see page 87). He said that when the passenger trains let people off they blocked the crossing over the street, so in the 1930s a new foundation and basement were built farther back, and ox teams hauled the building to its new site. Nicol said that because of this, the Liverpool station was the only one in the province to have a basement. According to the newspapers of the day, work on building the station began in December of 1904. A beautiful structure with classic lines, the station closed on January 25, 1981, seventy-six years to the day after the first passenger train left Liverpool for Halifax. It is today used as the Hank Snow Country Music Centre.

TRANSPORTATION: GETTING ABOUT

MILTON BLACKSMITH SHOP, C.1900

This photograph shows Augustus (Gus) Hemeon shoeing a horse at his blacksmith shop in Milton on the east side of the Mersey. The blacksmith shop was located near where a senior citizens' home is now operating. *Milton: Moments in Time* remarks that being a blacksmith ran in the Hemeon family. Gus Hemeon's grandfather was William Hemeon, who had a tanning business in Milton, and Gus's son George Thomas was also a Milton blacksmith. Augustus Hemeon was born in Milton in 1837 and died in 1908. His son George went into the blacksmith business as well. Except for eight years spent in the United States, George spent forty years owning and operating a blacksmith business in Milton. He died in 1951. To celebrate the importance of blacksmithing in Queens County, Milton has opened a blacksmith museum near the spot where the first mill was located at the falls.

TRAIN WRECK IN HUNT'S POINT, SEPTEMBER 16, 1936

One of the worst accidents in the history of the Halifax and South Western Railway occurred at Hunt's Point, west of Liverpool. On September 16, 1936, a train, having been delayed in Liverpool an hour due to the weather, left the station and rounded a curve in Hunt's Point where the tracks had been undermined by torrents of water. Engine number 5500 and four freight cars pitched off the tracks and down an embankment. Engineer Jimmy Hirtle and Fireman Manfred Hebb, of Bridgewater, jumped clear as the engine toppled over. Three passenger cars, carrying thirty passengers, miraculously stayed on the tracks, so that while Hirtle broke his back in the accident, there were no other serious injuries.

Newspapers reported that the engine was in a gully and lay on its back. Freight cars were crumpled up and piled on one another. "Rescuers arriving on the scene were appalled by the sight that met their eyes," a report said, "one

92   HISTORIC QUEENS COUNTY

that made it seem incredible for any one, let alone thirty, to escape death in the disaster." Dr. Jordan Wesley Smith arrived at the wreck shortly after it happened and administered first aid. For the next few days taxis transferred passengers around the wreck while trains shuttled back and forth between Hunt's Point and either Halifax or Yarmouth. The Hunt's Point railway station was removed on Thursday, June 29, 1961. This photograph is courtesy of the Queens County Museum and of William Sherod Crowell, Barrington, whose grandmother had it in her possession.

LIFE IN THE PORT MOUTON TRAIN STATION, C.1950S

Pictured is the train station at Port Mouton, built by the Halifax and South Western Railway and taken over by the Canadian National Railway a few years later. The station master during the 1950s and early 1960s was Raymond Goodwin, whose daughter Susan remembers what it was like to live in a train station. Sue—who today is co-owner of Sagor's Bookstore in Bridgewater—said that while she, her sister, and brother lived in the station there were four trains a day, two each way, two of them passenger trains and two freight. "I always felt it was my occupation to wave at the passengers, and I made my sister do it, too."

The little Port Mouton station had a garden with roses and peonies, kept up by Sue's mother, who was a nurse. It had a play house for the children, an old CNR shed dragged down the tracks for them to use. Sue said that while her bedroom overlooked the passing trains she wasn't aware of the noise. One of the trainmen always brought her a molasses cookie and she often got a chance to visit her grandparents in Lockeport and Pubnico, travelling either on the passenger trains or on a freight train caboose. Today she still loves trains and travels on them whenever she can.

THE MI'KMAQ BIRCH BARK CANOE, C.1900

First published in R.R. McLeod's 1908 book about the South Brookfield hunting and fishing lodge Pinehurst, this photograph shows Mi'kmaq men and two canoes they have made. Canoes were crucial to the Mi'kmaq and remain important to this day as a means of getting about the interior of Queens County. The canoe can pick its way among the rocks common to many of its lakes and travel to places impossible for other vessels to reach. They can be carried on portages, which today often follow trails used by the Mi'kmaq for hundreds of years. They enabled people to travel from the Bay of Fundy shore to the Atlantic on the South Shore through the interior of Queens.

In *Elitekey*, Ruth Holmes Whitehead, an expert on Mi'kmaq culture, points out that four basic canoe types were made: hunting, river, ocean-going, and war. She quotes an account by Nicholas Denys in 1672 that describes in detail the building of bark canoes, explaining how the largest birch provided sheets of bark the length of a canoe, inside which slats were placed for strength; bark was sewn with the roots of the black spruce, then sealed with the gum of the spruce (which in his account Denys called fir). Whitehead argues that the canoes were the "crowning achievement of Micmac material culture, in terms of workmanship and performance."

THE ROAD FROM LIVERPOOL TO THE NORTHERN DISTRICT, C.1900

This photograph, taken by A. Byron McLeod, shows the South Brookfield area at the turn of the nineteenth century. That road is now part of the Kejimkujik Scenic Drive, highway 8, which runs through Milton, Middlefield, South Brookfield, Caledonia, Harmony, Kempt, past the entrance to Kejimkujik National Park, Maitland Bridge, and on to Annapolis Royal.

There were no roads at first, of course. In 1798, Simeon Perkins said in his diary that three gentlemen from Nictaux, Annapolis County, had walked through the woods to Liverpool to propose cutting a road linking the two communities. Private subscribers had put up funds and the men wanted to form a cooperative venture with people in Liverpool to build the road. Liverpool residents—one of them being William Burke, the first person of European descent to settle in the Northern District—proved to be equally enthusiastic and work began. The road crossed the Medway at South Brookfield and went through the Brookfields to Nictaux, but when Caledonia evolved as the busiest part of North Queens, the route followed by Highway 8 through Caledonia, crossing the Mersey River at Maitland Bridge, became the main route.

Robert Johnson, who in 1999 compiled a history of South Brookfield for the North Queens Heritage Society to commemorate the 200th anniversary of the founding of Brookfield, said that at first the road would have been "only a blazed trail with a few crude bridges over some of the streams. An 1801 visitor noted that it was not wide enough for a horse and sleigh." Johnson went on to say that by 1837 the road had improved to the point where Tommie Waterman was running a weekly stagecoach between Liverpool and Brookfield, and soon after that all the way to Annapolis. The highway was finally paved in 1949 from Liverpool to Middlefield, in 1952 from Kempt to Cameron's Landing in South Brookfield, and in 1953 from there to join up with Middlefield.

THE FERRY FROM CAMERON'S LANDING TO MOLEGA AND GREENFIELD, 1883

Roads were notoriously unreliable in the Northern District as the nineteenth century drew to a close. As the Mi'kmaq knew, one of the best ways to travel the interior of Queens County was by boat. In the late 1800s a ferry began operating between Cameron's Landing, in South Brookfield, to Molega and down to Greenfield on Ponhook Lake. Johnson's history, *Brookfield in the Wilderness*, describes the route the ferry took when leaving a wharf near the present-day provincial picnic park at Cameron's Landing, avoiding the rocks on the way to Molega, then making for the west side of the Medway just above Greenfield, where a present-day Scout camp is located. This picture, dated 1883, was taken at Steamboat Wharf, Cameron's Landing, as the wood-burning steamer *Pioneer* gets ready to load passengers for Molega Mines. It is in the collection of the North Queens Heritage House.

    The ferry would carry approximately thirty people. An early issue of Caledonia's *The Gold Hunter* newspaper described a trip taken on the ferry, paying tribute to Elisha and Andrew More, two young North Queens men who operated the ferry with a boat they had had built. "Steaming out of the cove," the newspaper said, "we are soon in mid-channel, and pursue our way along the tree and shrub fringed shores of the river." It went on to say that the "stillness and solitude of the 'forest primeval' impresses us deeply." The ferry left Cameron's Landing every day except Sunday, the round trip to Greenfield and back costing forty cents.

FIRST TRAIN TO ARRIVE IN THE NORTHERN DISTRICT, 1903

It was a great day for North Queens when, on Dominion Day 1903, the first train arrived at South Brookfield, nearly two years before train service was established in Liverpool. People turned out along the route to wave the train on. The young woman in the white dress with the parasol in this picture is Olive Freeman, mother of Beryl Berringer, South Brookfield. Beryl Berringer provided this photograph, which was taken by R.R. McLeod.

The train route ran from Bridgewater to New Germany, then across to Caledonia. In June of 1903, before the opening of the line, the editor of *The Gold Hunter*, William Banks, took a ride on the Caledonia Branch Railway. He hitched up his horse Polly and drove over to Hemford, across the border in Lunenburg County, where work constructing the tracks and stations was underway. "The track was laid out beyond the town and the locomotive, with cars, was passing to and fro, whistling and ringing its bell at the crossings. The people seemed to be possessed of about all the joy they could stand." The editor said that when the line was opened the public would be invited to take a free trip on the new railway and that he had been asked to tell the people "that everybody and his best girl were coming to see the country."

In 1953, a big celebration was held in the village of Caledonia to honour a half century of rail service, but there will be no hundredth anniversary celebration. By 1975 the writing was literally on the wall. *The Advance* reported that the CN station in Caledonia was dilapidated. The waiting room, it said, still contained turn-of-the-century wooden benches and a pot-bellied stove, but a sign posted on the waiting room wall announced that application for authority to remove the agent and station building had been filed with the Canadian Transport Commission. The line closed on May 27, 1983.

HENRY HARPER'S BLACKSMITH SHOP, NORTH BROOKFIELD, C.1910S

Henry Harper arrived in North Brookfield from Jordan Falls in 1888 to establish his blacksmith business. In this photograph, courtesy of Henry's daughter Hilda, Henry is shown standing at the right. Hilda's brother Ernest is sitting on the horse, Jason is next to him, and Mirl, who worked with Henry, is shown in the doorway of the shop. Miss Harper, who still lives in the family home in North Brookfield, said that where the horse is standing there is a huge piece of slate with a hollowed-out part that Henry used to cool off the rims of the wagons after he had put them on. The large stone at the left in the photograph can still be seen in its same position at the North Brookfield corner. It was hauled down by a team of horses from a mill in Harmony.

Henry Harper worked at his blacksmith shop until just before his death at the age of eighty-nine in 1952. His marriage to Emma Butler of Liverpool produced a family of twelve, eight boys and four girls—all of whom except for Mirl were born in North Brookfield. Miss Harper said that her father could do anything: shoe horses and oxen, repair wagons, and build bear traps. "He could do anything that could be done with iron," she said.

AN OX-DRAWN HAY WAGON ON THE ROAD NEAR LIVERPOOL, C.1920S

Using oxen to pull loads and do work in the woods and around the farm was common along the South Shore and occasionally occurs today. People in the Northern District can still remember using oxen to take logs to Annapolis Royal, a journey which would begin early in the day with an overnight break at Mickey Hill, on the Annapolis Valley's South Mountain, to rest the oxen. Sometimes the teams went south, a trip to Chester taking about five days. Maurice Harlow, who was born in North Brookfield and who began keeping a diary in 1877, said he would leave home for Liverpool with a team of oxen and a wagon load of lumber at two in the morning, get to Liverpool by noon the next day, deliver the lumber and return to North Brookfield by evening on the third day.

Much of the work done with oxen now is ceremonial, as teamsters get ready for both the South Shore Exhibition in Bridgewater and the Queens County Fair in Caledonia. The oxen compete in pulls, sporting highly polished bells and carefully carved yokes made from yellow birch. The late Oran Veinot, a Caledonia farmer, was for a number of years the international ox pull champion, winning the title in ox pulls where he competed with teams from New England. This photograph was provided by Blair Douglas.

THE OLD ORDER CHANGES IN CALEDONIA: GARAGE AND BLACKSMITH SHOP, C. 1930

This photograph, taken by Les Henley, a North Queens photographer, looks west in the village of Caledonia, towards the Corner, so named because it marks the junction of roads to Hibernia, West Caledonia, and Harmony. On the left is a garage and on the right is a blacksmith shop. According to the *History of Caledonia*, written by Leone Smith, the garage was built in the early 1900s by Clifford Smith. After it burned another garage was built in its place by Jack McGuire and operated by him until his death. The spot is now a vacant lot. The blacksmith shop across the street was built by James Hunt in 1861. His sons Ezra and Jim took over the business from him. "They made shoes for horses and oxen," Leone Smith tells us, "and put them on. They made iron tires for wagons and did general iron work." She said the shop doors were almost always open and one could see an ox in the sling where the shoes were put on. "The ring of hammer and anvil and other sounds, and the many smells, were pleasing to the passersby. It was a gathering place, to watch, talk and listen." The shop was torn down in 1954.

Chapter 5

Daily Life

PEOPLE, SCHOOLS, STORES, CHURCHES, AND ASSOCIATIONS

ONE OF SYLVANUS COBB'S OLDEST DESCENDANTS OUTSIDE THE COBB HOUSE, 1934

Ella Jane Mulhall was the great-granddaughter and at one time the oldest direct descendant of Sylvanus Cobb, a founder of Liverpool and captain of the ship that took General Wolfe into the siege of Louisburg. Ella Jane was the daughter of Margaret (Freeman) and Captain Jesse Mulhall, and a cousin of D.C. Mulhall, a popular mayor of Liverpool and later high sheriff for the county. In 1933 the president of the Mersey Paper Company donated a monument to mark the historical significance of Cobb house, outside of which Ella Jane Mulhall is pictured in this photograph. Miss Mulhall, who was born in the house, was an honoured guest at the unveiling of the monument. She died in 1938. The Cobb house was destroyed by fire seven years later.

THOMAS HEAD RADDALL, AUTHOR

One of Canada's best-known and best-loved writers is Thomas H. Raddall, author of novels, historical essays, short stories, and articles. It was Raddall who wrote such popular books as *His Majesty's Yankees, Pride's Fancy, Halifax: Warden of the North, Roger Sudden,* and *The Governor's Lady,* all of which helped Nova Scotians and Canadians understand themselves and their history. Alan Wilson, who founded the history department at Trent University and who taught at a number of other Canadian universities, said he was often in Raddall's debt when he wanted to illuminate for young Ontario students a sense of what Nova Scotia and the Maritimes were all about, "for a passage read from Raddall caught them with its authenticity—its extraordinary familiarity with the ordinary ways of pioneers, soldiers, sailors, Imperial martinets, small townsmen and women, and above all, of shore people. There is a rich social history to be found in Raddall's pages."

Thomas Raddall was a part of the fabric of life in Queens County from the moment of his arrival in Liverpool in 1923 to work at the MacLeod Pulp and Paper Mill in Potanoc, Milton, to his death in 1994. He had a passionate interest in the history of the area, heading up the Queens County Historical Society and being instrumental in establishing the Simeon Perkins House Museum. His memoirs, *In My Time,* written in 1976, are indispensable for those interested in the history of Queens County. Thomas H. Raddall won honorary university degrees and Governor-General's awards, but in his memoirs he says that what he cherished most was a comment from the proprietor of a fishery business in Moose Harbour, who told Raddall he was proud to know him, "because you write about our own people and our own country, and you live here and you're one of us." The photograph on this page is used with the permission of Thomas H. Raddall's son, Dr. Thomas Raddall.

THE ACADEMY SCHOOL IN LIVERPOOL, ON FIRE, 1898

A paper written by John Leefe entitled "Early Education in Liverpool—A Sketch" says that the first recorded school in Liverpool was that of Amasa Braman, who opened the school mentioned in the diaries of Simeon Perkins on February 23, 1777. The first free school in Liverpool was the Academy School, shown in this photograph, built in 1867 at a cost of ten thousand dollars. At two o'clock on a February afternoon in 1898, the teacher of the junior department saw smoke coming up from the basement. News reports tell us she calmly took her children into another room and notified the principal, who quickly and without alarm organized the removal of all of the children from the building. By then, however, the fire had gotten out of control. Even though the town fire engine was brought to the site, it was impossible to save the school. By four o'clock the walls fell in, with four or five men on the ground floor jumping out of the windows to save themselves.

A second academy was built on the site in the same year. Since the academy was the only place in the county where provincial exams could be written for grades nine, ten, and eleven, students from all over the county, including North Queens, used to spend several days in the town to sit the exams, held in early July. After a hard week of studying and writing, the town would hold a band concert to celebrate the end of exams for the county's students.

DAILY LIFE

LIVERPOOL JUNIOR-SENIOR HIGH SCHOOL, 1945

This photograph, taken in 1945, shows the first junior-senior high school in Queens County. It opened in 1937 and was situated across from the second Academy School, which was demolished in the 1990s. The junior-senior high housed students from grades seven to eleven and was built after much public debate. In 1958 senior high students, now including grade twelve, moved out of the building and into a new school nearby, and in 1990 moved again, to the new Liverpool Regional High. When they vacated their building it became a junior high and the school in this picture became Liverpool Elementary. It ended its service as a school in 1996, when a new elementary school, named after beloved local physician Dr. John C. Wickwire, was opened. Today the building stands empty, though plans are afoot to turn it into a cultural centre.

CANADIAN LIGHT HEAVYWEIGHT CHAMPION TIGER WARRINGTON, C.1937

AT RIGHT

Former Canadian Light Heavyweight Boxing Champion Terrence "Tiger" Warrington was born in Mersey Point and learned the sport of boxing in the town of Liverpool. He quickly became something of a local boxing celebrity. Historian Armand Wigglesworth remembers being with the Boy Scouts, who were helping out with a boxing match at the Bristol Avenue baseball park (now the site of a supermarket). Wigglesworth says that while his opponent, a Cape Bretoner named Gus MacLellan, bested Warrington in the first two rounds, Tiger wore him down and won the match.

Garnie Seaman took over as Warrington's manager and before long they had run out of opponents in Nova Scotia. Liverpool fish plant owners Rosswell, Jerry, and Hubert Nickerson financed his foray into the rings of the eastern United States. Before long Tiger Warrington had demolished his opponents there. By the end of 1934 he was Canadian Light Heavyweight Champion. After he gave up his boxing career he moved back to the Liverpool area to live. He was voted into Nova Scotia's Sports Hall of Fame and died in 1978.

TIGER
WARRINGTON
C.1937

DAILY LIFE

THE HOME OF GILBERT KEMPTON, PHOTOGRAPHER, WITH FAMILY AND FRIENDS, C.1910

Gilbert Kempton was a Queens County photographer who was born in Milton in 1847 and who took up photography in 1892. He made a study of photography, used a succession of cameras, and set up a darkroom in his own home. Some of the most famous of the early photographs of Queens County were taken by Kempton. Much of his work was preserved by his son Gilbert Kempton Jr. In the picture shown on this page, Gilbert Kempton's house is in the background. In the foreground is a Chevrolet touring car with Harold Thompson, vice-president and manager of the Thompson Machinery Company, Liverpool, at the wheel. William J. Thompson, who was the president of Thompson Brothers, is in the passenger seat and behind him is his wife Minnie (Ford) of Milton. In the middle is Alice (Kempton) McCobb, daughter of Gilbert and Annie (Freeman) Kempton. Alice married Frederick Morton McCobb, a Massachusetts man, in 1905. Winnifred (Kempton) Thompson, another daughter of Gilbert Kempton, sits behind her husband Harold Thompson. Winnifred and Harold also married in 1905.

MAYOR AND SHERIFF D.C. MULHALL BY HIS HOME ON MAIN STREET, LIVERPOOL, C.1890S

Duncan Currie Mulhall was known to people as "D.C." In this photograph of his home on Liverpool's Main Street he is shown standing in the centre of the picture, which was taken by noted photographer N.D. Hammett. Not only was Mulhall mayor of Liverpool (first elected in 1898) and sheriff of Queens County (beginning in 1926), he was also a merchant, ship owner, ship builder, and lumberman. He was a director of the Liverpool and Milton Tramway, chairman of the school board, and president of the Queens County Historical Society.
The Mulhall family home was being built when D.C. Mulhall was born in 1866. The previous Mulhall house had been destroyed by the fire of 1865, a disaster which burned more than twenty buildings. In a note he wrote for Janet Mullins' book, *Some Liverpool Chronicles*, he said "On the day of my birth the frame for our new house was raised, the house in which, except for a few months, I have lived my entire life." The house still stands. D.C. Mulhall died in 1954 at the age of eighty-eight.

Aunt Liddy West, Mercy Hayden and Mercy's mother, c.1910

Photographer Gilbert Kempton took this photograph and left it to his son, Gilbert Kempton Jr., to explain what was happening. In his words, "The old lady whose picture Father Kempton placed in the tree was 'Aunt' Liddy West. The one in the doorway was Mrs. Hayden, mother of Freeman and Mercy. Mercy Hayden—who took care of her mother and Aunt Liddy—is by the gate. When I was a boy, I used to run errands and saw wood for Mercy (no charge—Orders from my father and mother) but she gave me ginger or molasses cookies, good thick ones. Mercy used to roast her coffee beans and grind them in her little coffee grinder. A good old soul and always good natured when I was around." The younger Gilbert Kempton, who spent much of his working career with Steel and Engine Products, Liverpool (formerly Thompson Brothers), died at the North Queens Nursing Home in 1968.

RESIDENCE OF FRANCIS COLLINS, LIVERPOOL, C.1880S

This summery photograph of Liverpool in the 1880s shows the home of Francis Collins, who died in 1890 after a long career as a respected Liverpool merchant. Francis Collins is shown on the extreme left, with George Snaddon, another Liverpool merchant, in the centre. George Snaddon died in 1935 at the age of ninety-four. His sister Charity, who went on to become active in education in Liverpool, is on the porch with Mrs. Frank Collins. In 1933, Liverpool celebrated Charity Snaddon's one-hundredth birthday; she died later that year. Miss Bertha Farish, daughter of Dr. Henry G. Farish, is at the extreme right of this picture. She went on to marry Charles V. McIntosh, a Liverpool hardware merchant, in 1904.

TRINITY CHURCH, LIVERPOOL, 1903

Governor Sir James Kempt laid the cornerstone for Trinity Anglican Church on July 13, 1821. A year earlier the government had granted a request that a parish be set up in Liverpool. A building committee was established and land was obtained from Hallett Collins and Benjamin Knaut. (Collins' son Enos became one of the wealthiest men in North America.) The church opened in 1822; markings on a shingle discovered in 1909 said the church had been built by the Halifax Casket Company, with William Spike the principal architect.

Trinity Rector C.R. Elliott tried to imagine the church as it was when it opened. He said it would be hard to recognize the present church as the same building, as it had grown "more venerable than old, more gracious than antiquated, and like many people more beautiful as the years go by." In a history of the church he asked people to picture the building when it opened in 1822. He said it was a plain building with an unprotected entrance on the west end, with three banks of pews with two aisles, all pews being boxed and gated. Heating was by means of stoves and lighting by oil lamps.

J.E. BARSS' CASH GROCERY STORE, C.1890S

The store to the right of this picture belonged to James E. Barss, son of Edward and Elizabeth Barss, who was born in Liverpool in 1831 and who died in 1913 at the age of eighty-two. When Barss was young he worked in the gold fields in both California and Australia, but he returned to Liverpool to become a merchant. In 1872 he went again to California for a period of ten years, returning to work in the gold rush in Queens County. For one period he was manager of the Parker and Douglas gold mine in Molega and also resumed running a store in Liverpool. When he died, the local newspaper noted that in politics he was a strong conservative, and added that "by his death the name Barss passes out of the town where it has been closely associated with the mercantile life of the place for 154 yeas, the first of that name coming here prior to 1760."

Next to Barss' store is that of Patrick. F. Butler, who later went on to be the proprietor of the Mersey Hotel, built in 1905. Butler was born in West Caledonia, son of early settlers who had come out from Kilkenny, Ireland. When he died in 1915, his son James took over as proprietor of the hotel. Next to Butler's is Samuel Rubin's store, which a few years later was being advertised as a menswear store, selling collars of the latest types, ties of the newest patterns, hosiery, underwear, hats, caps, and more at the most reasonable prices obtainable. Across the street a Liverpool woman and her son wait in a carriage.

GEORGE SNADDON'S STORE IN LIVERPOOL, C.1910

PHOTOS AT RIGHT

George Snaddon was a prominent Liverpool merchant who had been born in Port Medway in 1841. The exterior view of his store shows the Mersey Hotel on the corner opposite, built after the Thorndike Hotel burned to the ground in the same spot in December of 1902. The same fire burned Snaddon's previous store, the second store he had lost to fire. When the store shown in this picture burned on March 25, 1914 in a fire that took an entire block of stores, George Snaddon retired. The location was taken over by the Royal Bank, which built a brick building in its place. The interior view shows some of the items that Snaddon's store sold: groceries, fine china, glass, crockery and furniture, kerosene lamps, and other house wares, plus a small selection of tobacco.

THE LIVERPOOL CADET BAND, 1905

Marching bands were important in Queens County. Liverpool had its Liverpool Cadet Band, Caledonia its Caledonia Citizen's Band, and North Brookfield its North Brookfield Brass Band. This photograph shows the Liverpool Cadet Band sitting on the front steps of the Mersey Hotel in 1905. It played at numerous social and public functions, including Queen Victoria's Diamond Jubilee celebrations, and had the honour of leading a procession when the first train arrived in Liverpool. It was sometimes called the Weld Cadet Band, due to the fact that a wealthy benefactor, George W. Weld of Boston, supported the band. Weld visited Liverpool on his yacht in 1903 and was taken with the band, promising to provide the instruments required to equip it completely. The instruments arrived in Liverpool in November of 1904 and were put on display in the storefront windows of N.S. Wetmore and Sons. Liverpool continues to have an active band today, supported by the Bowater Mersey Paper Company.

THE CALEDONIA CITIZEN'S BAND, 1908

The Caledonia Citizen's Band, shown marching at the Caledonia corner in 1908, was organized by W.H. Banks, editor of the local weekly newspaper *The Gold Hunter*. Banks used to hold band meetings in the printing offices of the newspaper. Assisting with the band was Barney Arenburg of Lunenburg—called "Professor Arenburg" by the band members. The band's first official engagement was to play at a carnival in Lunenburg. The newspaper also reported wistfully of the time the band gathered to serenade Charles L. and Maude (Patterson) Mott on the night of their marriage in 1903. When Mott died in 1955, he was one of the last two surviving charter members of the band, and the last to be playing in the band.

The band eventually bought its own quarters, the former Caledonia school house north of the Corner. In August 1905, W.H. Banks editorialized that buying its own building was "a move in the right direction. The band boys work at their business in the day time, and practice in the evening, foregoing very often their own business, and should be encouraged as an organization in every way possible." The mortgage on the building was burned in 1924. Over the years, the band gave concerts, raised money through oyster suppers, played at pie socials and concerts, and marched in parades.

OLD SCHOOL HOUSE, MILTON, DATE UNKNOWN

This old school house in Milton was abandoned by the time this photograph was taken. In the middle of the nineteenth century public education really took hold in Nova Scotia, resulting in the building of 164 schools in 1865 alone. A system of inspectors went around each county assessing the quality of education.

Apparently, apart from in Liverpool and Mill Village, educational matters were not faring well in Queens County. In 1865, the school inspector found "the interests of education almost wholly neglected." A typical comment for Eagle Head was that it "has a house up and boarded, too small for the section and too near the road. Found it without trustees." However, he said, "the world moves, the day dawns, and a bright future is at hand." Change was coming quickly as public, free schools were established. In South Queens at the end of April 1865, there were 19 schools with just over 900 students. By October 1865, there were 23 schools, 1041 students. The inspector was also able to report that, as to outhouses, "there has been an alternation for the better."

MILTON'S ACADEMY SCHOOL, BUILT IN 1850, BURNED IN 1918

In 1850 the community of Milton built itself a fine new school, which it named the Academy School. Armand Wigglesworth's series on Queens County tells us that it included a high school. It was of an unusual design in that assembly room upstairs was made available to community groups for concerts and theatrical productions. The school's first headmaster was Nicholas Smith, who went on to be principal in Liverpool, and one of its teachers was Ralph Wetmore, who later went to Harvard and became chairman of Harvard's botany and biology departments.

On the morning of April 28, 1918, the school burned. Milton lumberman John Morton, who wrote about the fire in his diary, said he was twelve when the doors of the school first opened. "I attended school there two years under Andrew Willard, an unprincipled Yankee," Morton said, "and many a hiding he gave me. Some I probably deserved." Outside of his meanness, Morton said, Willard was a good teacher.

ETHEL MCLEOD, ON A VERANDAH IN MILTON, 1911

Life in the early 1900s seemed somehow more relaxing than life a century later. In this photograph Ethel McLeod is shown sitting on a hammock on the verandah of the family home, the Jason McLeod house in Milton, in 1911. Ethel's father Jason was a brother of the writer R.R. McLeod of South Brookfield, and father of Northern District doctor A.C. McLeod.

A couple of years earlier, Ethel had sent a postcard from Liverpool to her sister Mabel in Milton in which she begged off from a walking party planned for the evening, saying arrangements had been made for her to stay in Liverpool that night. What is striking about the note is that it was sent by mail in the morning by a person confident that it would be delivered before evening.

By 1914, Ethel was teaching the intermediate grades at school in Milton, a position she eventually left to marry George Farish Doggett. A news account of her wedding said: "The many gifts testified to the high esteem in which the bride was held in her home town, where she had been for some years one of Milton's most valued and efficient school teachers." Mabel, also a teacher, married Victor N. Thorpe, who himself became a school principal in the Annapolis Valley and eventually a lawyer and politician.

MILTON'S MARGARET MARSHALL SAUNDERS, AUTHOR OF *Beautiful Joe*, **1940**

One of the best-loved of all Canadian animal stories is *Beautiful Joe*, a story about an abused dog. The author of that story, Margaret Marshall Saunders, was born in Milton in 1861. In 1953 the village, along with the Canadian Historic Sites and Monuments Board, honoured her memory by unveiling a plaque near her birthplace. Guest speaker at the occasion was Watson Kirkconnell, President of Acadia University, who said that *Beautiful Joe* was the first Canadian book to sell over one million copies and probably the only one to have been translated into eighteen foreign languages. The plaque was unveiled by Edith Raddall, wife of author Thomas Raddall and a second cousin to Saunders.

Margaret Marshall Saunders was the daughter of a Baptist clergyman, Rev. Edward Manning Saunders, who was also a writer and editor. Margaret went to schools in Nova Scotia, Scotland, and France and for a time taught school, wrote articles, and travelled. In 1893 she entered *Beautiful Joe* in a competition sponsored by the American Humane Society for a book with the theme of intelligent sympathy for animals. She won. Her father advised her to turn down the $200 prize money and copyright the story instead, which she did. She published several more books but none as popular as *Beautiful Joe*. She died in Toronto in 1947.

THOSE WHO OPENED UP THE NORTHERN DISTRICT HONOURED IN 1899

A century after William and Mary Burke made their way to the wilderness of what was to become Brookfield, the community of South Brookfield celebrated their memory. Three thousand people, including a band from Mahone Bay, gathered on that day in 1899 on the knoll near where William and Mary had built their first cabin, and a replica of that cabin was erected on the actual site. This photograph shows that replica. Shown also are some local people relaxing with a few of the band members. Left to right a century ago are Harry Eisnor, Mahone Bay; Linda Dolliver, Caledonia; Allister Lantz, Mahone Bay; Josephine Dolliver, Caledonia; and Ralph Dolliver, Caledonia.

One of the most popular souvenirs of that day was this photograph of Mary Burke, who had died at the age of eighty-eight in 1856. The celebration had been organized by R.R. McLeod, writer and native son, who addressed the throng in an elegant speech in which he said of Mary that her life was no primrose path. With four children, she "followed her husband up the river to the spot where we are now assembled." All was forest and streams, "no roads, no neighbours, no farm, no school nor church." McLeod said she was scantily supplied with cash but richly endowed with energy and hope, and her family became a model for all pioneers. It fell to Mary to organize the home and walk to Liverpool to obtain supplies, a walk she also made for the births of her next four children so that she could be cared for by other women.

R.R. McLeod also said he hoped that when another century had been completed, there would be another celebration on the same spot "by men, women and children of our kindred and our spirit, intent upon perpetuating the sturdy virtues and useful lives of the pioneers of the Northern District." In 1999, the community of South Brookfield came together at the same location to celebrate the two hundredth anniversary of William and Mary's arrival. The people of the Northern District had kept faith with McLeod's hope.

Robert Randall McLeod, the Bard of Queens County, c.1903

One of the greatest of Nova Scotia's writers at the turn of the last century was R.R. McLeod, graduate of Harvard, author of a standard history of Nova Scotia, celebrated naturalist, poet, lawyer, geologist, photographer, educator, astronomer, and minister. McLeod was born in Westfield and grew up in South Brookfield, son of Ann, the daughter of Captain Josiah Smith, who moved inland from Liverpool, and of James B. McLeod, a Liverpool shipbuilder who moved inland to farm. R.R. McLeod was born in 1841, the ninth child of thirteen in the family.

His family includes a niece, the writer Grace McLeod Rogers, who was the first woman to earn a Master of Arts degree in Nova Scotia and the first woman governor of Acadia University, and her son Norman McLeod Rogers, who was Minister of National Defence in the wartime cabinet of Mackenzie King.

McLeod was largely self-taught, reading classics after the daily work was done. He worked on the family farm, then walked to Liverpool to be a sailor. At the age of twenty he had saved enough to go to Horton Academy in Wolfville; he hiked there and studied during the winter of 1860. That spring he worked as a log driver and earned enough to pay for a term at Harvard, where he studied literature and the classics. He also took classes in theology, becoming a Unitarian minister, and studied law. After seven years as a minister in Massachusetts, he passed his bar exams and became a lawyer. He also grew interested in geology and studied natural history in Mexico, learning much about mining in the process. That brought him back to Nova Scotia, where gold mining was underway. He returned to Brookfield (there was little distinction between the communities of North and South Brookfield in those days), where he engaged in mining and writing, producing the monumental work *Markland or Nova Scotia*, a history of the entire province.

When R.R. McLeod died in 1909, the *Halifax Herald* called him a distinguished Nova Scotian and an effective and fearless reformer. "He had the prophet's passion for justice and righteousness and was a persistent and uncompromising opponent of wrong and an aggressive fighter for the common good." This photograph appeared in a 1904 issue of *Acadiensis*, devoted to the history of Queens County.

The N.F. Douglas General Store, Caledonia, c.1910

The year 2000 saw the 125th anniversary of the N.F. Douglas general store in Caledonia, still both a thriving business and a tourist attraction, complete with a museum of the store's early history. By the turn of the century the store was being run by Nelson F. Douglas, who had inherited it from his father, Milton, who had first opened a store in Caledonia in 1875. The store shown in this photograph was built in 1907 in the prime location on the Caledonia corner, the site of the area's first school. The stables on the right of the store are for customers' horses. Gas lighting was installed in the store in December 1913—"Campbell's Scientific Acetylene Gas Lighting Plant," with twenty-four lights, first of its kind in the country. By 1919 the store had its own electric lighting plant and was even transmitting power to the Alton House next door.

When Nelson F. Douglas died, the business was run by his children, Perry, Lee, Viola, Helen, and Dora, until Perry and Lee gradually assumed the running of the store. From there the business went to Lee's son, the second Nelson F. Douglas, who expanded the business to more than double its size in 1990. He died in 1992 and his son Blair, who has served as president of the international hardware dealers association, runs it today as a unique combination of an old general store and a modern Home Hardware dealership. Blair also owns and operates N.F. Douglas Lumber, one of the largest lumber mills in the Northern District.

MAURICE SCOTT'S POOL HALL AND BARBER SHOP IN CALEDONIA, C.1930S

In 1929, Maurice Scott was advertising in the newspaper that his ice-cream parlour was selling LaHave ice cream in pints or quarts; a full line of ginger ales, always on ice; syrups, fruit, and sodas. At that time he described his business as an ice cream parlour, confectionery, and grocery store. In 1930 his nearby home, once known as the Ing Middlemas house, burned. The next year, Maurice Scott built the shop shown in this photograph in the location where the house had been, just north of the Caledonia corner. The top of the building was a doctor's office, the front room at the bottom an ice-cream parlour and in the back was a pool hall plus his barber shop. Electricity reached Caledonia in 1930, and a new electric light can be seen at the front of the building. A power line had just been built from the Mersey power development near Indian Gardens to Caledonia. Two years later it was extended to West Caledonia, and after that to Harmony, Kempt, and Grafton.

This photograph was taken by Les Henley, who was born in Maitland Bridge in 1869. Henley, who never married, had a number of interests—photography was one, colouring black and white photographs was another, and grafting apple trees around the community was yet another. It is said that he travelled around in a 1929 Ford and was a wild driver. Henley died at the age of eighty in 1949.

THE NORTH QUEENS FRUIT PACKING COMPANY LIMITED, CALEDONIA, C. 1920S

One of the sometimes forgotten facts about Queens County is that the Northern District was once an important apple-producing area. The farm of W.S. Crooker had over three thousand trees, with the apples being produced mostly for the English market, sometimes going by steamer from Annapolis Royal. By 1891 the northern district produced sixty thousand bushels of apples. In 1908 farmers established the North Queens Fruit Packing Company in order to obtain the best prices for fruit, and built a rail spur to connect with the main line. In 1921 the company did such things as pack a railway car of potatoes for Cuba and a carload of apples for England. By1945, when the once-prosperous apple exporting business had faded, the Queens County Co-operative Company was established, eventually selling farming implements, groceries, furniture, appliances, seeds, feed, and clothing. It operated with a board of directors and lasted until the 1980s.

The building shown in this picture was built in 1913 and is now on grounds owned by the Queens County Fair Association. On a tour of the warehouse in 1915, *The Gold Hunter* editor found a busy place: "Today North Queens has a fine warehouse in operation, a credit to the district and to the progressiveness of our farmer friends." The photograph is in the collection of the North Queens Heritage House.

CANNING FACTORY, CALEDONIA, C.1931

The drumlins which dot the interior of northern Queens County were quickly established as farms, after being settled in the early 1800s. Agriculture became a mainstay of economic life in the area and at one time it was described as the breadbasket of Queens County, shipping excellent quality flour to Liverpool. As a part of the agricultural boom, a canning factory was established at Caledonia in 1930. The building was put up by May and in the summer it was running with between twenty-five and fifty employees. A report in *The Gold Hunter* said that by August the plant was producing 100 cases of string beans per day, totalling 25,000 cases for the season. By October it was canning pears from the Annapolis Valley and making plans to run all winter, canning apples in one gallon tins. The next year it canned beans, pears, plums, beets, and sauerkraut, but by 1932, partly due to the depression, only portions of a large order from Winnipeg could be filled and the plant closed soon after.

THE PINE GROVE SCHOOL, C.1930S

This photograph shows the Pine Grove School in Caledonia, built during the years 1905-1906 with N.F. Douglas and Delbert Annis acting as contractors. When built, it had an attractive bell tower at the top, now removed as the old school passes its days as a private residence.

From the beginning, the pine grove behind the school for which the school was named was considered a feature, and a history of the school spoke with pride of the school's playground, considered at the time to be one of the best in the province. At first the playground was a half acre in size, but additional land was bought in the 1920s and a sports field was built. Maple trees were later planted along the front of the school. The school had two large classrooms, one for the primary department and one for the advanced grades. The building pictured above replaced a school that later housed the Caledonia band and that was eventually torn down to make way for a credit union. The community's first school was built on the site of the present-day N.F. Douglas store. All of the schools in the surrounding area were closed in the 1950s and 1960s, when school consolidation saw a rural high school and an elementary school built in Caledonia.

BUSSING CHILDREN TO SCHOOL IN THE NORTHERN DISTRICT, EARLY 1940S

PHOTOS AT RIGHT

This busload of happy children on their way to school shows a mode of transportation that is a far cry from that used today. Harry Ball, ninety-four in 2001, drove these children to the Central Caledonia school, located opposite the entrance to the road into the Whiteburn gold mines. He picked them up in Hibernia, settled in the 1830s by people from Ireland, and delivered them to the school, used today as a private residence.

The second photograph shows the same children deposited safely at the school. Harry, the first bus driver in the Northern District, can still name each of the children in the photograph. In the bus photo, the two little girls in front wearing the same outfits are Margaret and Edna Woodworth, with their sister Helen behind. They lived on the Mel Chute farm, about midway along the Hibernia Road between South Brookfield and Caledonia. Janine Rawding, daughter of Jim

BUSSING CHILDREN TO SCHOOL IN THE NORTHERN DISTRICT, EARLY 1940S

and Ada Rawding who lived near the Christopher Lakes, is to the left. The other girl in the back is Jeanette Chute, to the right of Helen. Earl and Gerald Selig are in the back, on the right, while Malcolm and Byron Chute are on the left.

THE CENTRAL CALEDONIA SCHOOL, 1940S

The Methodist Church and Parsonage, Caledonia, c.1910

The two pictures on this page show a Methodist church and parsonage, both in use today, in the village of Caledonia. In the early days of the village there was a common house of worship on the site of the present-day fair grounds, but when that was disbanded the Wesleyan Methodists decided to build their own. In 1864 George Middlemas, son of one of the original settlers of Caledonia and the first child born in Caledonia, provided land and work began. It continued for five years and cost $1,270. A 500-pound bell was installed in honour of George Middlemas in 1897.

By 1866 Caledonia had its own minister, Rev. E.B. Moore, who rented accommodations in the village. In 1876 a house on the Caledonia corner belonging to Joseph Harlow was purchased for $800 for use as a parsonage, the deed stating that it was for the "sole use of the Methodist minister." It is still in use as the United Church manse, the occupant at the present time being Rev. Natalie Buchanan, daughter of Senator John Buchanan, and her husband John McManamon. The photograph of the church was produced by the N.F. Douglas company as a postcard; both are from the Tim McDonald collection.

OFFICE OF *The Gold Hunter*, CALEDONIA, C.1900S

The Gold Hunter was an outstanding weekly newspaper published in the village of Caledonia for over fifty years, between 1888 and 1941. At one time Caledonia was said to be the smallest village in Canada to publish a weekly newspaper. In *We Have Held Our Own,* historians Jim Morrison and Lawrence Friend note that whatever a person's prominence, all fell under the watchful eye of William H. Banks, editor of the newspaper. "It catalogued the local news of everyday people and provided the residents with their own glimpse of the world outside." Banks had come to Caledonia from Annapolis County, his printing plant piled on a wagon pulled by a team of four horses, after being burned out in Annapolis three times. He was probably lured by the gold rush.

Morrison and Friend wrote that William H. Banks died in 1910 but that his son George, who also sold cars and ran a store in Caledonia, became editor and kept that position until fire destroyed the newspaper office in 1941. They point out that the paper was a strong booster of Caledonia and North Queens, and quote an editorial from 1919 that says, "Stop knocking, you pessimists, and join the procession for a bigger, better and brighter Caledonia. The larger the prosperity for Caledonia, the better for the whole district and county. The men and women who are lifting the world upward and onward are those who encourage and boost." When the newspaper office burned, Banks carried on job printing in Liverpool and died in 1944. George and Frances (Harlow) Banks from Harmony were the parents of Pauline, the wife of Premier Henry Hicks. *The Gold Hunter* office, shown in this photograph, was located next to the Baptist Church and was replaced in 1910 by the building which used to house the newspaper, moved to this site from its location near where the current post office stands. This photograph belongs to the North Queens Heritage House collection.

DAILY LIFE

DR. A.C. MCLEOD MAKES THE ROUNDS OF SOUTH BROOKFIELD BY BUGGY, C.1910

Dr. Albert C. McLeod was born in South Brookfield in 1874, son of Jason McLeod and nephew of the author and naturalist R.R. McLeod. Albert grew up in Milton after his father bought a pulp mill at Cowie's Falls and a paper mill at Rapid Falls. He attended Acadia University, taught school for a number of years, then studied medicine at Dalhousie, graduating in 1903. After practicing briefly in Liverpool he moved to Caledonia, where he bought the practice of Dr. W.H. Cole and served the district as a doctor until 1938, when he turned his practice over to Dr. Harry Smith of South Brookfield.

Dr. McLeod had also earned a degree in optometry and after retiring from medicine continued as an optometrist until the late 1960s. A story in the provincial press in 1969—the year he celebrated his ninety-fifth birthday—described him as the oldest practising optometrist in Canada, and the only surviving member of his 1903 graduating class at the Dalhousie Medical School.

THE SCHOOL AT SOUTH BROOKFIELD C.1930S

TOP RIGHT

The people of South Brookfield were proud the day their new school opened in 1932 atop a hill overlooking the South Brookfield corner, just metres from where R.R. McLeod at one time had his home. The school was built in a colonial style, with two classrooms inside covered in varnished native hemlock and sporting patterned metal ceilings. In the basement were the furnace, bathrooms, and an area for gymnasium activities. Water for the building was fed by gravity from a well up the hill behind the school. News reports of the day said the hall of the school would even have the wonder of a drinking fountain. The school cost six thousand dollars and was built by Arthur Boucher, of Liverpool. One of the teachers at this school was J. Murray Beck, who went on to become a distinguished Canadian political scientist and author. This photograph was taken by Harry Ball.

THE SCHOOL
AT SOUTH
BROOKFIELD,
C.1930S

THE
SCHOOL
HOUSE AT
MOLEGA,
C.1890S

This attractive little school house with its small tower was built in 1889 in Molega, which is on the northwestern end of Ponhook Lake in the Northern District. Gold was discovered in Molega in early 1888 and the area quickly became a boom town. All of the children in this picture moved there with their parents, who came to work in mines with names like the Minneapolis, the Parker and Douglas, the Caledonia, the Blue and the John McGuire. By 1890, the population was more than a thousand and the community had general stores, a meat business, and hotels. A study of place names undertaken by the public archives suggests that the name Molega came from Malaga, by which the community was sometimes known, referring to a Spanish mining town. During this time, in the absence of decent roads, a wood-burning steamer named the *Pioneer* carried passengers and freight between Molega, Cameron's Landing in South Brookfield, and Greenfield. A photograph of that steamer can be found in chapter four.

NOTED FARMER, HUNTER AND SPORTSMAN W.S. CROOKER, 1904

This photograph appeared in 1904 in an issue of the journal *Acadiensis*, devoted entirely to Queens County. W.S. Crooker is shown as he came out of the woods with a moose he had shot. Crooker, also a wild game commissioner, owned one of the finest farms in the district, a farm which is still in the Crooker family. He was important in the apple growing industry in North Queens; according to the Morrison history of the Northern District, in 1886 W.S. Crooker planted one thousand apple trees of different varieties, giving him some three thousand trees to tend. He was born in 1830 and died in 1905, the year after this photograph was taken.

Chapter 6

Through Good Times and Bad

SPORTS, LEISURE, CELEBRATIONS, AND HISTORIC EVENTS

CAMP COMFORT, RAPID FALLS, MILTON, C.1900

This photograph shows Liverpool residents camped for the weekend at Camp Comfort, located near where the Acadia Pulp Mill had its buildings at Rapid Falls, at the upper end of Milton. Harley Walker, who has written extensively about the history of Milton, remarks that it was common for people of that era to hop the Liverpool and Milton tramway, which ran up the west side of the Mersey, then crossed the river on a bridge at Rapid Falls. Walker believes that Camp Comfort was connected with the operations of the Acadia Pulp Mill. *The Advance* of June 1, 1898, reported that "a moonlight excursion to the Pulp Mill on the Tramway will take place on Friday evening, June 3rd," noting that music would be provided by the Liverpool Cornet Band.

QUEEN VICTORIA'S DIAMOND JUBILEE, JUNE 22, 1897

In the months leading up to the Diamond Jubilee of Her Majesty Queen Victoria, High Sheriff L.C. Drew called all loyal citizens of the county to meetings to help plan the big day. The managing committee was chosen and went to work, arranging for both events and decorations. This photograph, taken by N.D. Hammett, shows a series of arches over Main Street in Liverpool, with the Thorndike Hotel at the left. The town was particularly proud of the evergreen arches, which the press said were most tastefully constructed and very much admired.

The jubilee turned out to be an historic day. Besides the townspeople there were five thousand visitors to Liverpool. "The town was full of people; there were more people in it than there ever were before, or perhaps ever will be again," reported the local newspaper. They came from throughout the county and from outside the county. Both the Liverpool and Milton tramway and Captain Ryan's tug, plus other boats, brought school children down from Milton. Beginning at six in the morning cannons were fired and bells were rung; there was even a sixty-gun salute. By 8:00 A.M. Ballast Cove, off Fort Point, was the centre of activity, with whaler, skiff, dory, tub, and canoe races, plus a greased-pole competition. At 10:30 there was a grand street parade led by the Liverpool Cadet Band, with school children, the Temperance Society, and fraternal organizations taking part. The parade left from the Academy School, wound along Main Street to Fort Point, and returned to Bridge Street, where the school children sang the national anthem.

At noon the cutter HMS *Osprey*, sent to Liverpool by the federal government to help with the celebrations, fired off a royal salute, assisted by the dredge *Canada*. The afternoon was given over to sports, with foot races, high jumps, pole vaulting, putting shot, and water races, plus potato sack, barrel, and bicycle races, and finally a tug of war. There was another parade in the evening, with horses and bicycles, then an enormous fireworks display, for which the managing committee had spent thirty-five dollars. The fireworks were set off from the little island that today sits forlornly to the west of the harbour bridge.

SOLDIERS LEAVE LIVERPOOL FOR VALCARTIER, 1914

On August 20, 1914, at two o'clock in the afternoon, this unit of soldiers from Queens County left the Bristol Station at Liverpool on the Halifax and South Western Railway bound for Valcartier, Quebec. In the front is Major (later Colonel) Frederick Samuel Lampson Ford from Milton, a medical doctor who went to school in Milton and Liverpool and who received his medical degree from the University of Maryland. The previous night, Major Ford had joined the townspeople of Liverpool at the Opera House, where he and others made speeches describing the role of medical and surgical staff during wartime. The meeting raised funds to help equip a hospital ship.

The men in this photograph were members of the No. 2 Clearing Hospital of Liverpool unit. Just seven days after the unit left Liverpool, orders were given for it to take charge immediately of the stationary hospital at Camp Valcartier, described in a dispatch as a fine, commodious building. The regiment, with five practicing physicians on its roster as well as several medical students, was four days later given the honour of being chosen to go to the war front as the clearing hospital for the entire Canadian contingent. The newspapers said only one clearing hospital—regarded as the most important medical unit in active service—was allowed, and that "the little South Shore town of Liverpool may well stand proud of this latest honour that has been conferred upon it." Dr. Ford was promoted to colonel in 1916 and was seriously wounded at Vimy in 1917. He was the first Canadian soldier to be awarded the CMG medal (Companionage of the Most Distinguished Order of St. Michael and St. George) for bravery on the battlefield, bestowed at Buckingham Palace by King George V. Dr. Ford died in 1944.

CELEBRATING THE END OF WORLD WAR ONE IN LIVERPOOL, 1918

Monday, November 11, 1918 was a day of celebrations in Queens County. This picture shows the crowds outside the Liverpool Town Hall hours after news arrived that the great war had ended. Everything that would make a noise was pressed into service. Whistles blew loudly and continuously, bells on all of Queens County's churches rang out, and flags flew everywhere. Processions of automobiles and carriages decorated with bunting and carrying rejoicing townspeople wound through Liverpool, reported *The Advance*, "and in every way in which it was possible to give expression to general satisfaction and rejoicing, that expression was certainly given in no stinted measure." That night, the Opera House at the rear of the Town Hall was the scene of a number of patriotic addresses. "The greatest of all wars belongs to the past, and a new era has begun for the world."

BALL GAME IN THE EARLY 1900S, AND LIVERPOOL'S FAMOUS LARRUPERS, C. 1939

PHOTOS AT RIGHT

Liverpool and the sport of baseball have a long and storied history together. This game pictured here took place in the early 1900s. The location was the Bristol Athletic Grounds in Liverpopol, now the parking lot of a supermarket. The game may well have been the big Dominion Day game of 1904, played between Liverpool and Bridgewater, which the newspapers reported resulted in the defeat of the Bridgewater team by a score of 23-11. "At the close of the game," the newspaper said, "both teams were escorted to Sheppard's by Mayor Mulhall, where ice-cream was served." Sheppard's was a grocery and ice cream business located just before the bridge on the Bristol side of the Mersey, run by William J. Sheppard, clerk of the county court for many years.

CROWDS WATCH A LIVERPOOL BASEBALL GAME, 1900S

Liverpool has often been described in the provincial press as a baseball town, partly because of the success of the legendary Liverpool Larrupers, who won the Nova Scotia Senior Baseball Championship in 1938. The team got its name from the sports editor of the *Halifax Herald*, who wrote after one game that the Liverpool team had "larruped"—or thrashed—another team. The greatest of the Liverpool Larrupers was Danny Seaman, called by Halifax newspapers the Babe Ruth of the Maritimes. Equally adept at baseball or basketball, Danny Seaman was invited to try out for major league teams, founded Liverpool's annual high school basketball festival, and was named to the Sports Hall of Fame. He died in 1973 in Antigonish, while refereeing a basketball game. The town's baseball field is named after him.

In this team photograph, Danny Seaman is in the front row at the left. Next to him, left to right, are Howie Martin, Fran Mouzer, Moe Bowers, Bruce Thorbourne, Kit Wells, Jack Rudderham, and Al Young. In the back row, left to right, are Vic Winters, Louie Thorbourne, Billie Rice, Nels Deveau, Lloyd Young, Carly Walthers, Fred Dagley, and Artie Wells.

LIVERPOOL'S FAMOUS LARRUPERS, C.1939

SETTING OFF FOR A SUNDAY SCHOOL PICNIC FROM DR. FARISH'S HOUSE, C.1900

Gilbert Kempton took this photograph of a group of mothers and their children as they set off on a Sunday School picnic. They are travelling on a wagon owned by Balcom's Express and are setting off from in front of Dr. Henry G. Farish's house. Dr. Farish, whose father was a doctor in Yarmouth, came to Liverpool in 1850 and practised medicine continuously in Liverpool for fifty-six years, retiring in 1906. The carriage was from the large livery stable owned by Willis Balcom, who drove the coach between Liverpool and Bridgewater before the railway arrived. He died in 1938 at the age of ninety-four.

A. Harris McLeod, who grew up in the McLeod house on Shipyard Point, asks "who can forget that wonderful picnic ground, Hill's Grove [now Pine Grove Park], visited annually by hundreds of Sunday school children and adults? Picture a beautiful summer afternoon and a gathering of children, their parents and teachers, at Shipyard Point, where boats are provided to take them across the river to the grove, there to enjoy the long looked-forward-to Sunday school picnic," he said, writing in Janet Mullins' *Some Liverpool Chronicles*. Games and races provided the afternoon fun and when the call to supper was heard, the tired and hungry rushed to picnic tables, "laden with all the good things one could wish to eat. Supper over, songs are sung and stories told till the sun begins to set."

LEISURE ACTIVITIES AT BALLAST COVE, OFF FORT POINT, 1900S

PHOTOS AT RIGHT

When you walk around Fort Point today you find a relaxing, grassy park with benches overlooking the water. The point of land from which the people of Liverpool used to watch for privateers has had many uses over the years, many of them associated with the defence of the town, but there was always a recreational component. These photographs, from the early 1900s, show the waters off Fort

ROWING RACES OFF FORT POINT, 1900S

Point, in Ballast Cove, being used when work was done. The first shows rowing races and the second canoeing in bark canoes.

One of Liverpool's early doctors, Henry G. Farish, wrote a series of reminiscences about life in Liverpool, saying of Fort Point that it was "the trysting place of the young men and maidens; here also the old father and mother with their children, hand in hand, sauntered, particularly on Sunday evenings after service, to inhale the pure air from off the ocean after being half suffocated with the oppressive heat of the churches…it is a peculiar habit with us even now to have our stroll to this cool resort, to sit upon the benches provided, and probably enjoy a little gossip or discuss the merits of the sermon."

AN OUTING IN BIRCH BARK CANOES, OFF FORT POINT, 1900S

139   THROUGH GOOD TIMES AND BAD

The Great Liverpool Fire of 1895

The great Liverpool fire of 1895 began early in the morning of September 8, 1895, in a building known as the Old Bakery. *The Advance*, which lost its own building, called it the most destructive conflagration that ever visited the town of Liverpool. Sixty-six buildings, including nineteen businesses, were destroyed that day. The three photographs shown here include a number of the buildings before they were destroyed by the fire, a view of Main Street looking in the same direction after the fire, and a view from the bridge looking towards Main Street at the corner where the post office now stands. Sitting on the safe in one picture is Norman Reinhardt, with his son (also Norman) beside him. The jeweller Thomas Bird is behind and to the left.

As soon as the alarm was raised the town's steam fire engine poured water on the bakery but the flames spread, taking the two buildings between the bakery and the water, and jumping across the street to burn a large, three-storey wooden building known as Jubilee Hall. The flames were so intense at this time that the steamer engine was moved across the bridge, though several lengths of hose were burned. Fire moved in several directions, burning a blacksmith shop, residences, a flour store, and a block of other stores. It took more houses, a molasses shed, and several more stores. N.D. Hammett's photographic studio went up in flames. Destroyed were a meat store, a boot and shoe store, a hardware store, Mulhall's grocery, Hallett's tailors and clothiers, two stores owned by N.S. Wetmore, a jewellery store, and the London Fruit Store. Although a gale fanned the flames, efforts of fire fighters stopped the fire just before it got to a group of large wooden buildings.

In the other direction, flames were working along the south side of Main Street, destroying Thomas Bird's jewellery store, the McNutt grocery store, *The Advance* building, plus a barber shop and a butcher's. Also burning was the largest building in Liverpool, once known as the Music Hall, the lower portions of which were occupied by a bank and a general store. The fire reached and burned the Trilby Hotel (see page 38). A burning shingle from the Trilby lit on the spire of the Congregational Church, and though frantic efforts were made to blow up the spire with dynamite, fire destroyed the church.

SURVEYING THE AFTERMATH OF THE GREAT FIRE OF 1895

LOOKING TOWARDS MAIN STREET FROM THE BRIDGE, 1895

The fire of 1895 was the second of three major fires to hit Liverpool. The first was in 1865, when fire began in a barn used as a stable for Royal Mail coaches during a long drought, and ended up destroying some twenty buildings, including two churches. Liverpool was hit again in 1914, when several buildings burned.

THE THORNDIKE HOTEL BURNS, DECEMBER 1902

Milton lumberman John Morton recorded in his diary on December 16, 1902, that early Saturday morning the Thorndike Hotel "took fire and burned to the ground. The inmates had difficulty to save their lives." Yet another destructive fire had struck Liverpool, also burning, for the second of three times, George Snaddon's store, seen in this Gilbert Kempton photograph as a smouldering ruin next to where the Thorndike had been.

The hotel had had a short life. It had been built where the Trilby Hotel stood, after the Trilby had been destroyed in the great fire of 1895, and burned just seven years later. The hotel had been admired. A travel feature published in a Boston newspaper in 1897 said "we arrived at Liverpool late at night, and were driven at once to Hotel Thorndike—a new and thoroughly modern house," a picture of which was published in the paper.

FAMOUS AUTHOR ZANE GREY FISHES FOR TUNA AT LIVERPOOL, C.1924

Queens County has always been a magnet for people who love the outdoors, attracting its share of famous hunters, fishers (both male and female), photographers, campers, hikers and "sports"—as many Americans who came to the county for recreation in the early 1900s were called. Zane Grey, whose most famous novel *Riders of the Purple Sage* sold fifteen million copies and was made into a movie, took part in tuna fishing off Liverpool. In the 1920s and 1930s giant bluefin tuna were plentiful in Liverpool Bay. This photograph shows Zane Grey, left, in Liverpool, being proclaimed world tuna fishing champion in 1924. The photograph was provided by the family of the late photographer Harry MacLeod, and is courtesy the DesBrisay Museum.

In his autobiography, Thomas Raddall writes about Zane Grey as an American sportsman who found huge tuna on the coast near Liverpool. Grey "made an immense fortune out of saddle-and shoot-'em-up novels of the Wild West," Raddall said, "but personally liked to ride a luxurious yacht and kill big fish with hook and line. After his encounter with what some of our fishermen called 'horse mackerel' he went away to the Pacific, where fish were just as big and the weather much more comfortable." On May 13, 1929, the newspapers reported that Zane Grey was to fish at Greenfield. They said that Laurie Mitchell (who had been the first manager of the Kedgemakooge Rod and Gun Club) was on Grey's staff and was now living in Los Angeles, and had arrived to make arrangements for a salmon fishing trip. Mitchell had just completed a year-long cruise to Australia and New Zealand with Grey in his yacht *The Fisherman* and was bringing him to fish in June on the Medway at Greenfield, after which they would fish in Newfoundland and return to Liverpool in August for tuna fishing.

ON THE RIVER, LIVERPOOL, 1905

This looks to be an idyllic scene. The man and woman in the boat in the foreground are enjoying the calmness of the Mersey River. In the background, the salvage vessel *Help*, with a diver, sounds for the site of the Liverpool railway bridge. The photograph was taken by Gilbert Kempton in 1905.

The Mersey used to be something of a boating paradise, with boats able to navigate upstream to wharves and docks along the way. The first of the two bridges spanning the river from Bristol Avenue to the town proper had mechanisms that allowed the bridge to be turned so that boats could get through. Local historian and author Armand Wigglesworth remembers riding on the second bridge as it turned its span out of the way. When the present bridge was built, it was hoped that a drawbridge system would be built in, but one was not, much to the disappointment of townspeople.

143 THROUGH GOOD TIMES AND BAD

A PICNIC AT WHITE POINT, C.1900S

A faded photograph of a group of young adults on a picnic at White Point hints at the kinds of leisure activities popular at the turn of the last century. A social note in the *The Advance* of July 6, 1904, describes just such a picnic: "On Friday last a jolly crowd of 31 young people drove to White Point for a picnic outing as the guests of Miss A.A. Mollins. Notwithstanding the fog and the lack of sunshine the drive was so pleasant that even the most morbid could not have resisted the contagion of good fellowship. A bumping drive of ten miles produces only one result, and the wrecked condition of the picnic tables at about one o'clock told the tale. Walks, games and more walks filled the afternoon, and really it was surprising how much pedestrianism was practiced and enjoyed by some. As the twilight began to fall, the return began. Liverpool was reached shortly after nine, a parade of the streets was made, and all dispersed after voting that Miss Mollins was 'all right' and 'a jolly good fellow.'"

A PICNIC AT PINE GROVE PARK, MILTON, C.1900

PHOTO AT RIGHT

This undated photograph was taken at Pine Grove Park, then called Hills Grange or Hill's Grove Park. Today the park is owned and maintained by the Bowater Mersey Paper Company Limited. In the earlier years of Queens County, a picnic was one of the best ways to have fun. There were church picnics, picnics to celebrate special days, picnics by families and by communities. This photograph does not identify either the people or the occasion, but the camera has captured several young women and a couple of young men relaxing at the park. The Mersey River can be seen through the trees.

Milton lumberman and merchant John G. Morton, who was born in 1838, chronicled much about life in Milton and Liverpool in a set of diaries he kept throughout his long life. On Dominion Day, 1908, he noted that there had been a great turnout in Liverpool and that after a baseball game, he and his family "were invited by Mayor Mulhall and ex-mayor Hendry to the picnic in Hill's

PICNIC AT PINE GROVE, C.1900

Grove, where we met the elite of Liverpool, guests from abroad, and quite a number of the first people of Milton, and had a most enjoyable time. Duncan generally does things right, and when he starts in goes to win. The whole was a great success. Four or five naptha launches with boats in tow, and horses and carriages, took all the guests from the grounds, with band playing and flags flying. Everyone delighted. Hill's Grove is now owned by D.C. Mulhall and Geo. S. McClearn, who have spent considerable money in improving the grounds, trimming up the trees, and repairing the road, with most commendable public spirit, as the grounds are intended for public enjoyment."

THE MEDWAY RIVER FLOODS, JANUARY 1956

When the Medway River's banks broke in January of 1956, Delbert Crooker's General Store in Mill Village, shown in this photograph, was inundated with water. Newspaper reports said the flooding was the worst in the memory of its oldest residents, and noted that the Crooker store had three feet of water running through it. Flooding also affected Chester Veinot's store, and in a bit of wit, *The Advance* said the parking lot would accommodate boats only. Several families in the Mill Village area had to evacuate their homes, while the fire station was under water and held in place by cables to trees.

Flooding was due to continuing rains and melting snow. Millions of dollars worth of damage was caused around the province by what was termed the most disastrous January thaw in history. Greenfield and Bang's Falls were cut off and the Harry Freeman sawmill destroyed, and the highway running between Liverpool and Caledonia was impassable at South Brookfield. Both Westfield and Albany New were also cut off from the outside world by the floods.

CANOEING ON THE MEDWAY RIVER IN SOUTH BROOKFIELD, C.1900

This idyllic photograph shows a man and child in a birch bark canoe on the Medway, in South Brookfield. One writer, Stephen A. Davis, has pointed out that Europeans adopted three major items used in eastern Canada by the Mi'kmaq—the canoe, the toboggan, and the snowshoe.

The early history of the canoe is obscure, it being generally accepted that it was first used by the Algonquins of northeastern North America. Evidence of its existence can be found in the petroglyphs, or rock drawings, at Kejimkujik National Park and National Historic Site. Descriptions of canoes date from Jacques Cartier's time, and a good contemporary account can be found in *Maritime Firsts*, which said the canoe was "distinctively fashioned by the Mi'kmaq, its centre sides curved upward in order to remain stable in open water. White birchbark sown together with split spruce root and caulked with spruce gum, produced an excellent, lightweight vehicle for use along Maritime rivers, lakes and coastal waters."

Celebrations and Sports Activities a Century Ago, 1899

When thousands gathered in South Brookfield a hundred years ago to attend celebrations recognizing the first settlers in North Queens, greased log-rolling in the water, shown in the photograph below, was just one of the competitions. The day was organized by R.R. McLeod, who lived just a few hundred metres from the site of Burke's cabin. There were many events, including a royal salute, shooting competitions, canoe races, log rolling, hammer throws, baseball, a tug of war, and a horse trot. Booths were set up on the grounds near the first settler's cabin, there was a ceremonial Mi'kmaq encampment nearby, and a festive air, echoed later by a similar celebration in 1999.

Greased log rolling at South Brookfield celebrations, 1899

Ceremonial Mi'kmaq encampment, South Brookfield, 1899

PIE SOCIAL AT NORTH BROOKFIELD, C.1890S

People gather at the hall in North Brookfield before the turn of the century for a pie social. The woman in the white dress in the centre is Matilda Fiske Dailey. The man to her left, with the beard, is James Slocum Dailey, her husband, and beside him is Jamie Dailey, their son, one of their twelve children. James Slocum Dailey ran a large lumber mill on the Rosette Road, near Westfield, and was a descendant of the original James Daley (the spelling had changed), who came into the Northern District just after William Burke.

The pie socials were hugely popular events. The ladies in the community—mainly the single ones—would bake pies, which would be auctioned off to the highest bidder. Whomever won the bidding could eat the pie with the young lady who baked it, satisfying both the requirements of romance and of fund raising. Sometimes there would be box lunches prepared and auctioned in the same manner. For variation, the community held a Poverty Social, where people dressed in rags, and organizers charged fines for real and imagined infractions of the rules. Women were fined one cent for arriving without an apron, two cents for wearing a hat with flowers or feathers, five cents for wearing powders or paints, one cent for having an ornamental hair pin, five cents for wearing a new dress and three cents for wearing a wool dress; men were fined a cent for wearing black boots, a cent for wearing a watch not a "Waterbury," five cents for a stand up collar, two cents for patent leather shoes, two cents for young whiskers, three cents for flirting, and a cent for wearing perfume. A committee would collect the fines and introduce strangers, plus introduce and look after "bashful fellers." The photograph is courtesy of Judy and Eric Cole, Rosette Road, Westfield.

AT THE NORTH QUEENS EXHIBITION, NOW THE QUEENS COUNTY FAIR, 1905

In 1886 Matilda Fiske Dailey wrote to her brother Samuel in California that "the people of North Queens last summer built a large wooden building where we could hold our agricultural exhibitions. It was erected at Caledonia on the same ground where the old Baptist meeting house stood. We held our exhibition the 13th and 14th of October. Supposed to be about 2000 persons present. At one time they counted about 200 teams on the grounds, besides all that were at the stables."

The two-storey wooden building Matilda refers to is shown in the photograph above, taken in 1905, and continues to be used for that purpose a century later. One of the first agricultural exhibitions in Queens County had been held in Harmony in 1880, but in 1886 the association purchased permanent quarters in Caledonia for ten dollars. The fair has been held there ever since. In 1935 it became the Queens County Fair, serving the whole county. Today it is one of the few remaining genuine agricultural fairs, as it is held after harvest each September. The letter Matilda wrote and the exhibition season ticket are in the possession of her great-granddaughter Judy Cole of Rosette Road, Westfield. The photograph is courtesy of Freda Smith, South Brookfield. The booth in the picture with the "Band" sign was used by the Caledonia Citizen's Band to raise funds for its activities.

Greenfield's Laura and Laurie Wamboldt, Queens County guides, c.1937

The first woman guide in the province was Laura Wamboldt, shown here with her husband Laurie in a log rolling competition in Columbus, Ohio. During the 1930s and 1940s, Laura and Laurie Wamboldt were international stars. They competed and performed in sportsmen's shows in the winter months, spent the spring guiding for fishermen in Nova Scotia and the fall guiding for hunters. The first of the shows was held in Boston in 1935, where guides from Nova Scotia were hired to demonstrate their skills for those attending the big boat and sports show at Boston Gardens. The shows caught on and over the next few years Nova Scotia guides were competing in log rolling, wood chopping, canoe tilting and tub racing in a number of United States cities, sometimes before crowds of fifteen thousand people.

Laura and her friend Viola Peters from Bear River were enormously popular, two beautiful young Nova Scotia women dressed in two-piece bathing suits. Laura and Viola once earned an extra six hundred dollars for being able to drive a pair of ostriches attached to two-wheeled sulkies in a series of races. "That was the way it was," she said. "Whenever they had something no one else would do, they would say Laura could do it. And I would." Laura and Laurie also competed in the Nova Scotia Guides Association meets, Laura becoming pistol shooting champion in competition against male guides. The annual guides meets are now held at the Twin Lakes Campground in Hibernia, Queens County.

Laura and Laurie moved from Molega Mines to Greenfield in 1947, buying land at the place where Ponhook Lake and Little Ponhook Lake meet. They established Ponhook Lodge, today a prime summer destination for tourists and campers. Later on they bought Ponhook Rim, a strip of land which runs out into Ponhook Lake. Today Laura, a widow, lives in a summery house on the shores of Ponhook Lake while the lodge and property business are run by her sons, Ted and Bill. She provided this photograph.

GUIDES OF THE NORTH WOODS, C.1952

The photograph above shows two Kedgemakooge guides, Fred Lewis in the stern of the canoe on the left and Noble Fancy in the stern of the canoe on the right, while their clients display the fish they have caught. In *Guides of the North Woods*, Mike Parker writes that Fred Lewis was the head guide at Kedge Lodge and a veteran of thirty years there. "His duties," Parker writes, "were to ensure that a sufficient number of guides were available for hire, sports and guides were properly matched, daily hunting areas designated, equipment maintained and complaints investigated. In his spare time he was chauffeur, ferry-boat operator, baggage handler and resident fire chief."

Kedge Lodge used to hire sixteen guides at the height of the hunting season, the book says, and twenty sports would be at Kedge for a week's hunting at any given time. Ninety per cent of the guiding business was for sports from the United States. Noble Fancy, the other guide in this picture, started guiding in 1945 and eventually became a provincial game warden. The photograph is used with permission of Mary Lee Mahoney, daughter of Fred Lewis.

LODGE AND CABIN INTERIOR, MERRYMAKEDGE, NOW PART OF KEJIMKUJIK NATIONAL PARK, 1942

PHOTOS AT RIGHT

This lodge and cabin were a part of Minard's Cabins, now the site of Merrymakedge Beach, in Kejimkujik National Park and National Historic Site. The cabins used to go for three dollars a day or eighteen dollars a week. This one and six others like it were made of logs, and featured open fireplaces, verandahs, and showers; they sat on two hundred acres of land with almost a mile of lake frontage. The photograph of the cabin is courtesy of the Public Archives, and that of the lodge is from the collection at Kejimkujik National Park.

The cabins were begun in 1908. *Guides of the North Woods* notes that Mert Minard of nearby New Grafton and William Cummings of Maine built the cabins to cater to the sports lured to the area by its superior hunting and fishing.

After Mert died and William returned to Maine, the cabins were taken over by Mert's brother Charles, until fire in the 1940s destroyed the main cabin. At one point the area was bought by the Catholic Church for a retreat, but in 1953 a Maitland Bridge resident named Arthur Merry purchased the property and renamed it Merrymakedgie, a name which lives on today (without the "i") in the popular public beach and swimming area at Kejimkujik.

There was a main lodge with hardwood floors and a big kitchen, several tenting sites, trails, a cabin cruiser for rides on a lake, and a store. The land was taken over for the national park, which was established in 1969. Parker quotes Arthur Merry as saying that the enterprise was not a real money-maker. "I was just in it to make a living because I loved doing it. We loved that country so bad, every stick and stone of the place. I haven't been back to it. It was a pleasant business in so many ways; you'd meet lovely people."

Image Sources

Cover, photo by Gilbert Kempton, courtesy Queens County Museum

Title page, courtesy Queens County Museum

p.viii, courtesy Kejimkujik National Park

p.xii, courtesy Tim McDonald

p.xiv, photo by E.G.L. Wetmore, courtesy Nova Scotia Archives and Records Management

p.xx, photo by Clara Dennis, courtesy Nova Scotia Archives and Records Management

p.xxi, courtesy North Queens Heritage House

p.1, photo: Royal Canadian Air Force, courtesy Nova Scotia Archives and Records Management, Halifax

p.2, photo by Gilbert Kempton, courtesy Queens County Museum

p.3, 4, 5, courtesy Queens County Museum

p.6, courtesy Nova Scotia Archives and Records Management

p.7 (both), courtesy Queens County Museum

p.8, courtesy Tim McDonald Collection

p.9, courtesy Queens County Museum

p.10, photo by Will Thorpe, courtesy Nova Scotia Archives and Records Management

p.11, photo believed to be by Alister Harlow, courtesy Tim McDonald Collection, in Queens County Museum

p.12, courtesy Tim McDonald Collection

p.13 (top), first published in *Acadiensis*, 1904, courtesy South Shore Regional Library

p.13 (bottom), courtesy Queens County Museum

p.14, photo by Aaron Rhodes, courtesy Queens County Museum

p.15 (both), courtesy Queens County Museum

p.16, courtesy Tim McDonald Collection

p.17 (both), courtesy Marilyn Clarke

p.18, courtesy Queens County Museum

p.19, first published in Acadiensis, 1904, courtesy South Shore Regional Library

p.20 (both), courtesy Queens County Museum

p.21, from collection at Kejimkujik National Park, used with permission of Mrs. Freda Smith

p.22, courtesy Nova Scotia Archives and Records Management

p.23 (both), courtesy Beryl Berringer

p.24, courtesy Blair Douglas

p.25, 26, courtesy Tim McDonald Collection

p.27, courtesy Eugene Penney

p.28, courtesy Nova Scotia Archives and Records Management

p.29 (top), courtesy Sandra Rowter

p.29 (bottom), photo by Les Henley, courtesy Eugene Penney

p.30, courtesy Judy and Eric Cole

p.31, courtesy Queens County Museum

p.32, courtesy Nova Scotia Archives and Records Management

p.33, courtesy Queens County Museum

p.34, courtesy Nova Scotia Archives and Records Management

p.35, photo by E.G.L. Wetmore, courtesy Nova Scotia Archives and Records Management

p.36, photo by Gilbert Kempton, courtesy Queens County Museum

p.37, courtesy Queens County Museum

p.38 (top), courtesy Tim McDonald Collection

p.38 (bottom), 39, 40, 41 (both), 42, 43, 44, 45, courtesy Queens County Museum

p.46 (top), photo by Gilbert Kempton, courtesy Queens County Museum

p.46 (bottom), first published in *Beautiful Queens*, 1903 and reprinted by the Queens County Museum

p.47, 48, courtesy Queens County Museum

p.49, courtesy Nova Scotia Archives and Records Management

p.50, courtesy Carol Doggett

p.51, photo by E.G.L. Wetmore, courtesy Nova Scotia Archives and Records Management

p.52, 53, courtesy Queens County Museum

p.54, courtesy Carol Doggett

p.55 (both), courtesy Tim McDonald Collection

p.56, courtesy Blair Douglas

p.57, courtesy North Queens Heritage House

p.58 (top), photo by Paul Yates, courtesy Kejimkujik National Park

p.58 (bottom), courtesy Blair Douglas

p.59 (top), photo by Dewey Photographic Studio, Chatham, NB, courtesy DesBrisay Museum

p.59 (bottom), courtesy Tim McDonald Collection

p.60 (both), courtesy North Queens Heritage House

p.61, courtesy Queens County Museum

p.62, photo by Gilbert Kempton, courtesy Queens County Museum

p.63, 64, courtesy Nova Scotia Archives and Records Management

p.65 (top), by Gilbert Kempton, courtesy Queens County Museum

p.65 (bottom), courtesy DesBrisay Museum.

p.66, 67, courtesy Queens County Museum

p.68, photo probably taken by Aaron Rhodes, courtesy Nova Scotia Archives and Records Management

p.69, courtesy Queens County Museum

p.70, photo first published in *Acadiensis*, 1904, courtesy South Shore Regional Library

p.71, 72, courtesy Queens County Museum

p.73 (top), photo by Gilbert Kempton, courtesy Queens County Museum

p.73 (bottom), courtesy Alan Wilson

p.74, courtesy Shirley Smith and North Queens Heritage House

p.75 (both), courtesy Queens County Museum

p.76, courtesy North Queens Heritage House

p.77 (both), photos probably by L.G. Swain, courtesy Queens County Museum

p.78, courtesy Beryl Berringer

p.79 (top), courtesy North Queens Heritage House

p.79 (bottom), courtesy Beryl Berringer

p.80, courtesy Queens County Museum

p.81, courtesy Eugene Penney

p.82, courtesy Tim McDonald Collection

p.83, courtesy North Queens Heritage House

p.84, courtesy Tim McDonald Collection

p.85, photo by Gilbert Kempton, courtesy the Queens County Museum

p.85, photo by N.D. Hammett, courtesy Nova Scotia Archives and Records Management

p.87, courtesy Queens County Museum

p.88, photo by Gilbert Kempton, courtesy Queens County Museum

p.89 (both), photos by Gilbert Kempton, courtesy Queens County Museum

p.90, photo by Gilbert Kempton, courtesy DesBrisay Museum

p.91 (both), courtesy the National Archives of Canada

p.92 (top), courtesy the Queens County Museum

p.92 (bottom), courtesy William Sherod Crowell and the Queens County Museum

p.93, courtesy Carol Doggett

p.94, photo probably taken by A. Byron McLeod, published in *Pinehurst* or *Glimpses of Nova Scotia Fairyland*, 1908, and made available by Kejimkujik National Park

p.95, photo by A. Byron McLeod, first published in *Acadiensis*, 1904, courtesy of the South Shore Regional Library

p.96, courtesy North Queens Heritage House

p.97, courtesy Beryl Berringer

p.98, courtesy Miss Hilda Harper

p.99, courtesy Blair Douglas

p.100, photo by Les Henley, courtesy Eugene Penney

p.101, from the Clara Dennis Collection, courtesy Nova Scotia Archives and Records Management

p.102, with permission of Dr. Thomas Raddall Jr.

p.103 (top), courtesy Queens County Museum

p.103 (bottom), 104, courtesy Tim McDonald Collection

p.105, courtesy Queens County Museum

p.106, photo by Gilbert Kempton, courtesy Queens County Museum

p.107, courtesy Nova Scotia Archives and Records Management

p.108, photo by Gilbert Kempton, courtesy Queens County Museum

p.110, courtesy Queens County Museum

p.111, courtesy Nova Scotia Archives and Records Management

p.112, 113, 114, courtesy Queens County Museum

p.115, courtesy Blair Douglas

p.116, courtesy Nova Scotia Archives and Records Management

p.117, courtesy Queens County Museum

p.118, courtesy Nova Scotia Archives and Records Management

p.119, from the Clara Dennis Collection, courtesy Nova Scotia Archives and Records Management

p.120 (top), courtesy Queens County Museum

p.120 (bottom), courtesy Judy and Eric Cole

p.121, first published in *Acadiensis*, 1904, courtesy Kejimkujik National Park

p.122, courtesy Blair Douglas

p.123, photo by Les Henley, courtesy Eugene Penney

p.124, courtesy North Queens Heritage House

p.125, photo by Les Henley, courtesy of Eugene Penney

p.126, in the possession of Althea Banks, provided by Kejimkujik National Park

p.127 (both), photos by Harry Ball, courtesy Harry Ball

p.128 (both), courtesy Tim McDonald Collection

p.129, courtesy North Queens Heritage House

p.130, courtesy Beryl Berringer

p.131 (top), photo by Harry Ball, courtesy of Harry Ball

p.131 (bottom), courtesy Queens County Museum

p.132, first published in *Acadiensis*, 1904

p.133, courtesy Queens County Museum

p.134, photo by N.D. Hammett, courtesy Queens County Museum

p.135, 136, 137 (both), courtesy Queens County Museum

p.138, photo by Gilbert Kempton, courtesy Queens County Museum

p.139 (both), courtesy Queens County Museum

p.140, 141, courtesy Queens County Museum

p.142 (top), photo by Gilbert Kempton, courtesy Queens County Museum

p.142 (bottom), courtesy family of photographer Harry McLeod and DesBrisay Museum

p.143, photo by Gilbert Kempton, courtesy Queens County Museum

p.144, first published in *Some Chronicles of Liverpool*

p.145, 146, courtesy Queens County Museum

p.147, first published in *Acadiensis*, 1904

p.148 (both), courtesy Beryl Berringer and Kejimkujik National Park

p.149, courtesy Judy and Eric Cole

p.150 (top), courtesy Mrs. Freda Smith

p.150 (bottom), courtesy Judy and Eric Cole.

p.151, courtesy Laura Wamboldt

p.152, courtesy Mary Lee Mahoney

p.153 (top), courtesy Kejimkujik National Park

p.153 (bottom), courtesy Nova Scotia Archives and Records Management

Bibliography

Cole, Connie and Tim McDonald. *Milton: Moments in Time*. Yarmouth, N.S.: Connie Cole, 1995.

Davis, Stephen A. *Peoples of the Maritimes—The Mi'kmaq*. Tantallon, N.S.: Four East Publications, 1991.

Dennis, Clara. *More About Nova Scotia: My Own, My Native Land*. Toronto: The Ryerson Press, 1937.

Elliott, C.R. *Time to Remember: History of Trinity Church Parish, Liverpool, N.S., 1820-1970*. Liverpool, N.S.: 1970.

Fergusson, Charles Bruce. *Early Liverpool Days and its Diarist*. Halifax, N.S.: Bulletin of the Nova Scotia Archives and Records Management, 1961.

Flick, Don. *London Brook Lodge in Goose Hills*. Hantsport, N.S.: Lancelot Press, 1979.

Harlow, Maurice. *Diary of Maurice Harlow, 1877-1935*. In the collection of the North Queens Heritage House.

Jack, David Russell, ed. *Acadiensis*, Vol. IV, Number 2. April, 1904.

Johnson, Ralph. *Forests of Nova Scotia: A History*. Halifax, N.S.: Four East Publications/Department of Lands and Forests, 1986.

Johnson, Robert. *Brookfield in the Wilderness: A History of North and South Brookfield, Queens County, Nova Scotia, Commemorating the 200th Anniversary of the founding of Brookfield*. Caledonia, N.S.: North Queens Heritage Society, 1999.

Leefe, John. *Early Education in Liverpool—A Sketch*. Paper presented to the Queens County Historical Society, Liverpool, N.S.

Leefe, John and Peter McCreath. *Early History of Nova Scotia*. Tantallon, N.S.: Four East Publications, 1982.

Leefe, John, James Morrison, et al. *Kejimkujik National Park*. Tantallon, N.S.: Four East Publications, 1981.

Lawson, Amy B. *The Items: Diary of a Village: A view of life in Summerville Centre, Queens County, Nova Scotia, as published in The Liverpool Advance, 1935-1975*. Liverpool, N.S.: privately published, 1975.

Letson, E. Marguerite. *Port: A Short History of Port Medway, Nova Scotia*. Port Medway: Duncan Harper, Publisher, 1985.

Letson, W.A. *Beautiful Queens*. Liverpool, N.S., 1903, reprinted by the Queens County Museum, 1993.

Martin, J. Lynton. *This Land!* Halifax, N.S.: Nova Scotia Museum, 1972.

Masson, Sheena. *Paddle Lunenburg-Queens: An Adventure Guide for Canoeists and Kayakers*. Halifax, N.S.: Lunenburg-Queens Recreation Association, 1998.

McLeod, R.R. *Markland or Nova Scotia: Its History, Natural Resources and Native Beauties*. Toronto: Markland Publishing Company, 1903.

McLeod, R.R. *Notes Historical and Otherwise of the Northern District of Queens County*. Halifax: Nova Scotia Historical Society, 1912, reprinted by The Queens County Historical Society, 1996.

McLeod, R.R. *Pinehurst or Glimpses of Nova Scotia Fairyland*. Boston: The Bartlett Company, 1908.

Mersey Quarterly, Liverpool, N.S.: Bowater Mersey Paper Company Ltd., including: *The Historic Homes of Lower Main Street, Liverpool*, Summer 1985; *History of Brooklyn*, Summer 1970; *Liverpool in the Twenties*, Winter 1965; *Liverpool Street Names*, Winter 1968; *Markland Shipping Company Ltd.*, Fall 1954; *The Medway River*, Fall 1964; *The Old Port of Liverpool*, Summer 1964; *The Saga of Enos Collins*, Summer 1965.

More, James F. *The History of Queens County*. Halifax: Nova Scotia Printing Company, 1873.

Morrison, James and Lawrence Friend. *"We Have Held Our Own": The Western Interior of Nova Scotia, 1800-1940*. Ottawa, Ontario: Parks Canada, 1981.

Mullins, Janet E. *Some Liverpool Chronicles*. Liverpool: *The Advance*, 1941, reprinted by Lancelot Press for C.D. Hemeon, 1980.

Mullins, Janet E. *Liverpool Privateering 1756-1815*. Liverpool: Queens County Historical Society, 1936.

Mullins, Janet E. *The Liverpool Packet*. Liverpool: The Queens County Historical Society, undated.

Paul, Daniel N. et al. *People of the Dawn: Reclaiming History*. Mi'kmaq History Supplement in *Shunpiking*, Nova Scotia's Discovery Magazine, Halifax, N.S., October-December 2000.

Parker, Mike. *Guides of the North Woods—Hunting and Fishing Tales from Nova Scotia, 1860-1960*. Halifax, N.S.: Nimbus Publishing Ltd., 1990.

Parker, Mike. *Woodchips and Beans: Life in the Early Lumber Woods of Nova Scotia*. Halifax, N.S.: Nimbus Publishing, 1992.

Penney, Allen. *The Simeon Perkins House: an Architectural Interpretation 1767-1987*. Halifax, N.S.: The Nova Scotia Museum, Curatorial Report Number 60, 1987.

Raddall, Thomas H. *His Majesty's Yankees*. Garden City, New York: Doubleday, 1942.

Raddall, Thomas H. *In My Time: A Memoir*. Toronto: McClelland and Stewart Ltd., 1976.

Raddall, Thomas H. *Ogomkegea: the Story of Liverpool, Nova Scotia*. Liverpool, N.S.: Queens County Museum, 1983.

Raddall, Thomas H. *The Mersey Story*. Liverpool, N.S.: Bowater-Mersey Paper Company Limited, 1979.

Robertson, Barbara R. *Sawpower—Making Lumber in the Sawmills of Nova Scotia*. Halifax, N.S.: Nimbus Publishing and the Nova Scotia Museum, 1986.

Sack, Michael. *Mike Sack's Mi'kmaq Place*. www.accesswave.ca/~mtsack

Sheppard, Jonathan. *Nature's Gentleman: Robert R. McLeod*. Unpublished essay in the North Queens Heritage House, 1996.

Shireffs, J. William. *Gold in Queens County*. Caledonia, N.S.: North Queens Heritage Society, 1976.

Smith, C. Leone. *History of Caledonia, Queens County, Nova Scotia, 1820-1973*. Liverpool, Nova Scotia: Queens County Historical Society, 1997.

Smith, Zenas. *Diary*. Unpublished diary in the possession of Shirley Smith, Harmony.

Soucoup, Dan. *Maritime Firsts: Historic Events, Inventions and Achievements*. Lawrencetown Beach, N.S.: Pottersfield Press, 1996.

Tupper, F.F. *Historic Liverpool*. Published in Nova Scotia, 1944: No publication information available.

Waterman, Simeon F. *History of Middlefield*. Unpublished manuscript, undated, in the North Queens Heritage House, Caledonia, N.S.

Whitehead, Ruth Holmes. *Elitekey: Micmac Material Culture from 1600 AD to the Present*. Halifax, N.S.: The Nova Scotia Museum, 1980.

Wile, Janet. *A History of Greenfield, Queens County, Nova Scotia*. Typewritten manuscript, 1975.

Wilson, Alan. *My Mother and Thomas Raddall*. Unpublished memoir, 2001.

Woodworth, M. Marie. *The Early History of Port Mouton*. Liverpool, N.S.: The Queens County Historical Society, 1983.